INTERNET THEORY, TECHNOLOGY AND APPLICATIONS

INTERNET TELEVISION STREAMING, COPYRIGHT LAW AND THE AEREO SUPREME COURT DECISION

INTERNET THEORY, TECHNOLOGY AND APPLICATIONS

Additional books in this series can be found on Nova's website under the Series tab.

Additional e-books in this series can be found on Nova's website under the e-book tab.

INTERNET THEORY, TECHNOLOGY AND APPLICATIONS

INTERNET TELEVISION STREAMING, COPYRIGHT LAW AND THE AEREO SUPREME COURT DECISION

MEREDITH LANE
EDITOR

NOVINKA

New York

For permission to use material from this book please contact us:
Telephone 631-231-7269; Fax 631-231-8175
Web Site: http://www.novapublishers.com

Library of Congress Cataloging-in-Publication Data

ISBN: 978-1-63321-723-2

Published by Nova Science Publishers, Inc. † New York

CONTENTS

Preface		**vii**
Chapter 1	Aereo and FilmOn X: Internet Television Streaming and Copyright Law *Emily M. Lanza*	**1**
Chapter 2	Cartoon Network LP v. CSC Holdings, Inc.: Remote-Storage Digital Video Recorders and Copyright Law *Kate M. Manuel*	**19**
Chapter 3	Decision of the Supreme Court of the United States in the case of American Broadcasting Cos., Inc., et al. v. Aereo, Inc.	**37**
Index		**63**

PREFACE

This book discusses internet television streaming and copyright laws. It then discusses remote-storage digital video recorders and the copyright laws that go along with it.

Chapter 1 – Aereo and FilmOn X stream television programming over the Internet for a monthly subscription fee. Aereo and FilmOn's technology permits subscribers to watch both live broadcast television in addition to already-aired programming. Their use of this development in technology has triggered multiple lawsuits from broadcasting companies alleging copyright violations. These cases reveal not only multiple interpretations of copyright law and its application to new and developing technologies but also a possible "loophole" in the law, which some have accused Aereo and FilmOn of exploiting.

The Copyright Act of 1976 provides copyright holders with the exclusive right to control how certain creative content is publicly performed. Of particular interest to courts in recent cases against Aereo and FilmOn was the meaning of the Copyright Act's "transmit clause" that determines whether a performance is private or public and within the scope of the public performance right. Specifically, the courts have been divided as to what constitutes a "performance to members of the public" for the purposes of the transmit clause.

During the past two years, groups of broadcasters have filed lawsuits against Aereo and FilmOn alleging that the retransmissions of their programs by these companies have violated their right of public performance. While both FilmOn and Aereo use similar technology, the courts have disagreed about whether this technology infringes upon the copyright holder's right of public performance. In 2013, the U.S Court of Appeals for the Second Circuit in *WNET v. Aereo* affirmed the lower court decision ruling that the transmissions by Aereo did not infringe the plaintiffs' public performance right. However, district courts in the District of Columbia (*Fox Television Stations v. FilmOn X*) and California (*Fox Television Stations v. BarryDriller Content Systems*) have held that FilmOn's retransmissions did violate the right of public performance.

The Second Circuit held that Aereo's transmission of broadcast programs is not a public performance because Aereo is transmitting a copy of the program made by Aereo available not to the public at large but only to a specific subscriber. However, the D.C. and California district courts have disagreed with this interpretation. These courts have held that the retransmission by FilmOn of the broadcasters' copyrighted material is a public performance and therefore violates the broadcasters' copyright. For the D.C. and California district courts, the one-copy-persubscriber technology of FilmOn does not exclude the company from the public performance right when the service is transmitting the same underlying program to various subscribers.

These decisions, however, do not mark the end of litigation over these issues. The parties have filed appeals in the circuit courts, and in January 2014, the U.S. Supreme Court granted a petition for writ of certiorari filed by the plaintiffs (petitioners) in *WNET v. Aereo*. Additionally, two bills in the 113th Congress address issues related to Internet television streaming. These bills, the Television Consumer Freedom Act of 2013 (S. 912) and the Consumer Choice in Online Video Act (S. 1680), would enhance consumer choice regarding online television programming, a service marketed by both Aereo and FilmOn.

Chapter 2 – The time-shifting technologies that consumers use to record television programs as they are broadcast and to play them back later have long prompted allegations of copyright infringement from broadcast networks and movie studios. However, as the technologies have evolved and lawsuits against their manufacturers have been resolved, the nature of the copyright claims has changed. In 2006, broadcasters and studios sued Cablevision over its proposed remote-storage digital video recording service, which would allow consumers to record and play back broadcast content using Cablevision's facilities instead of in-home devices. Because the recordings were made at Cablevision's facilities and the playbacks were transmitted from there, content owners claimed direct infringement of their reproduction and public performance rights. Previously, copyright holders had claimed contributory or vicarious infringement by manufacturers of recording devices.

In 2007, a federal district court in New York found for the plaintiffs and enjoined Cablevision from operating its proposed recording service, holding that (1) the unauthorized buffer and playback copies made when recording broadcast programming were infringing reproductions, and (2) the unauthorized transmissions of playback copies to consumers were infringing public performances.

In 2008, the U.S. Court of Appeals for the Second Circuit reversed the district court. It found that neither buffer nor playback copies infringed content owners' reproduction rights. According to the appellate court, the buffer copies were non-infringing because they were embodied too briefly for fixation to occur and to count as "copies" under the Copyright Act. The playback copies were similarly non-infringing because Cablevision's customers, not Cablevision, created them. Additionally, the Second Circuit found that Cablevision's transmission of playback copies to consumers did not infringe content owners' public performance rights. The transmissions were non-infringing because Cablevision made individualized copies of every television show for each recording customer and customers could view only "their" copies.

Beyond clarifying the nature of infringing reproductions and public performances under the Copyright Act, the Second Circuit's *Cartoon Network* decision, coupled with the Supreme Court's subsequent denial of certiorari in the case, paves the way for Cablevision to market the first-ever remote-storage digital video recording service. This effect of the *Cartoon Network* decision could potentially be undercut by the parties' failure to allege contributory infringement, vicarious infringement, or fair use, as well as by the fact that the decision is binding precedent only within the Second Circuit. However, to the degree that courts in other circuits follow the Second Circuit, they may view remote-storage digital video recorders as successors to video cassette recorders and set-top-storage digital video recorders, protecting manufacturers of the latest time-shifting technologies from liability for copyright infringement.

Chapter 3 – This is the Decision of the Supreme Court of the United States in the case of American Broadcasting Cos., Inc., et al. v. Aereo, Inc.

In: Internet Television Streaming …
Editor: Meredith Lane
ISBN: 978-1-63321-723-2

Chapter 1

AEREO AND *FILMON* X: INTERNET TELEVISION STREAMING AND COPYRIGHT LAW*

Emily M. Lanza

SUMMARY

Aereo and FilmOn X stream television programming over the Internet for a monthly subscription fee. Aereo and FilmOn's technology permits subscribers to watch both live broadcast television in addition to already-aired programming. Their use of this development in technology has triggered multiple lawsuits from broadcasting companies alleging copyright violations. These cases reveal not only multiple interpretations of copyright law and its application to new and developing technologies but also a possible "loophole" in the law, which some have accused Aereo and FilmOn of exploiting.

The Copyright Act of 1976 provides copyright holders with the exclusive right to control how certain creative content is publicly performed. Of particular interest to courts in recent cases against Aereo and FilmOn was the meaning of the Copyright Act's "transmit clause" that determines whether a performance is private or public and within the scope of the public performance right. Specifically, the courts have been

* This is an edited, reformatted and augmented version of a Congressional Research Service publication R43359, prepared for Members and Committees of Congress, dated March 20, 2014.

divided as to what constitutes a "performance to members of the public" for the purposes of the transmit clause.

During the past two years, groups of broadcasters have filed lawsuits against Aereo and FilmOn alleging that the retransmissions of their programs by these companies have violated their right of public performance. While both FilmOn and Aereo use similar technology, the courts have disagreed about whether this technology infringes upon the copyright holder's right of public performance. In 2013, the U.S Court of Appeals for the Second Circuit in *WNET v. Aereo* affirmed the lower court decision ruling that the transmissions by Aereo did not infringe the plaintiffs' public performance right. However, district courts in the District of Columbia (*Fox Television Stations v. FilmOn X)* and California (*Fox Television Stations v. BarryDriller Content Systems*) have held that FilmOn's retransmissions did violate the right of public performance.

The Second Circuit held that Aereo's transmission of broadcast programs is not a public performance because Aereo is transmitting a copy of the program made by Aereo available not to the public at large but only to a specific subscriber. However, the D.C. and California district courts have disagreed with this interpretation. These courts have held that the retransmission by FilmOn of the broadcasters' copyrighted material is a public performance and therefore violates the broadcasters' copyright. For the D.C. and California district courts, the one-copy-per-subscriber technology of FilmOn does not exclude the company from the public performance right when the service is transmitting the same underlying program to various subscribers.

These decisions, however, do not mark the end of litigation over these issues. The parties have filed appeals in the circuit courts, and in January 2014, the U.S. Supreme Court granted a petition for writ of certiorari filed by the plaintiffs (petitioners) in *WNET v. Aereo*. Additionally, two bills in the 113th Congress address issues related to Internet television streaming. These bills, the Television Consumer Freedom Act of 2013 (S. 912) and the Consumer Choice in Online Video Act (S. 1680), would enhance consumer choice regarding online television programming, a service marketed by both Aereo and FilmOn.

Companies such as Hulu, Netflix, and Amazon have changed how many people watch television programming by offering on-demand, online streaming to their computers, mobile devices, and gaming consoles.[1] Aereo and FilmOn X also stream television programming over the Internet for a monthly subscription fee. Unlike the other companies, however, the technology of Aereo and FilmOn permits subscribers to watch both live broadcast television and already-aired programming without licenses. This development in technology has triggered multiple lawsuits alleging copyright violations by these companies. The litigation reveals not only multiple interpretations of copyright law and its application to new and developing technologies, but also a possible "loophole" in the law, which some have accused Aereo and FilmOn of exploiting.[2]

The Copyright Act of 1976 provides copyright holders with the exclusive right to control how their work is reproduced, adapted, distributed, publicly displayed, or publicly performed.[3] The issue before the courts in the lawsuits against Aereo and FilmOn X is whether a retransmission of copyrighted broadcasts over the Internet without a prior agreement with the copyright holder violated the copyright holder's right of public performance.

In 2012, the U.S. District Court for the Southern District of New York, in *ABC v. Aereo,* denied certain broadcasters' request for a preliminary injunction against Aereo.[4] The plaintiffs argued that Aereo's service of transmitting copyrighted television programs contemporaneously with over-the-air broadcasts violated their right of public performance. The defendant, Aereo, in turn argued that the performances were not public but private because each user could access only his/her specially made copy of the program. The district court agreed with Aereo's argument. That same year, the plaintiffs appealed to the U.S. Court of Appeals for the Second Circuit in *WNET v. Aereo.* The Second Circuit, in a split appellate panel, affirmed the district court decision ruling that the transmissions by Aereo did not infringe the plaintiffs' public performance right.

FilmOn X modeled its system on Aereo and its recent endorsement by the courts. However, FilmOn has not enjoyed the same legal success as Aereo, despite the similar arguments made by both the plaintiffs and defendant in the *Aereo* cases. In the 2012 case *Fox Television Stations v. BarryDriller Content Systems*, the U.S. District Court for the Central District of California found that FilmOn's retransmission of certain television programs violated the copyrights of several broadcasters.[5] In 2013, the U.S. District Court for the District of Columbia found, in *Fox Television Stations v. FilmOn X*, that FilmOn's retransmission of the plaintiffs' copyrighted programs over the Internet violated their right of public performance because FilmOn retransmitted copyrighted works to members of the public without the plaintiffs' prior permission.[6]

This report will examine the courts' interpretation of the public performance right in the context of the *Aereo* and *FilmOn* cases. The report begins with a discussion of the technology used by *Aereo* and FilmOn. The report then examines the public performance right, specifically the "transmit clause," in the Copyright Act. Next, the report discusses the interpretation of the transmit clause and public performance right by the courts in the Aereo and FilmOn cases. The report concludes with a brief overview of future litigation by these parties and related legislative proposals in the 113th Congress.

AEREO AND FILMON TECHNOLOGY

Competitors Aereo and FilmOn X use similar technology, with only minor distinctions but no legally meaningful differences, to retransmit broadcast television to their subscribers.[7] Both companies allow subscribers to view and/or record live broadcast programming. Unlike most other digital video recorders (DVR) that require a television, Aereo and FilmOn allow users to view programming on their computers or mobile devices, similar to services offered by Hulu and Netflix.[8] However, Aereo and FilmOn, unlike Hulu and Netflix, have not negotiated any licensing agreements with the content providers. Content providers have even accused Aereo of "stealing content" while Aereo has defended its service as a new player in the media market.[9]

In order to watch a program, the Aereo/FilmOn subscriber first logs into an account on the website. The subscriber then either selects to watch a program as it is aired or chooses to record a program that will be aired later.[10] When a subscriber selects to watch a currently airing program, Aereo/FilmOn transmits to the subscriber a webpage from which he/she can watch the television program at roughly the same time as the current broadcast. While viewing this program, the subscriber can pause, rewind, and record the program with the system retaining a copy until the subscriber watches it later. These features allow the subscriber to watch a program even after the over-the-air broadcast has ended. The Aereo and FilmOn systems, therefore, provide the functionality of both a television antenna and a DVR.[11]

When a subscriber selects to watch or record a program, the web browser sends a request to the Aereo/FilmOn application server.[12] The application server then sends information about the subscriber and the selected program to the antenna server. The antenna server allocates a specific antenna to that subscriber. These antennas receive the broadcast television channels, from which the subscriber selects the programming. Depending on the type of subscription, most of the subscribers are assigned a different antenna each time they select a program. However, no two subscribers are using a single antenna at the same time.[13]

The selected antenna then receives the incoming broadcast signal. The antenna server receives the data from the antenna and then sends it to another server where a copy of the program is saved to a large hard drive in a directory reserved for that particular subscriber.[14] Regardless of whether the subscriber has selected to watch or to record a program, the system streams the program from the hard drive copy of the program in the user's directory on the server.[15] The difference between the two viewing modes is when the streaming occurs: after six-seven seconds of programming has been saved on the hard drive for the "watch" option or when the subscriber chooses to view the program.

The courts have highlighted three technical details of significance.[16] First, Aereo and FilmOn assign individual antennas to each subscriber even if two or more subscribers are watching or recording the same program. Second, the system creates a separate copy of the program, stored in the subscriber's personal directory. Third, each subscriber can only access and watch the copy specifically made for his/her account. No other subscriber can view that particular copy.

1976 Copyright Act & Public Performance Right

The 1976 Copyright Act provides copyright holders with exclusive rights to control certain uses of their works.[17] These exclusive rights include "in the case of literary, musical, dramatic, and choreographic works, pantomimes, and motion pictures and other audiovisual works" the right to do and to authorize the public performance of the copyrighted work.[18]

The Copyright Act defines "public performance or display" as

> (1) to perform or display it at a place open to the public or at any place where a substantial number of persons outside of a normal circle of a family and its social acquaintances is gathered; or (2) to transmit or otherwise communicate a performance or display of the work to a place specified by clause (1) or to the public, by means of any device or process, whether the members of the public capable of receiving the performance or display receive it in the same place or in separate places and at the same time or at different times.[19]

The second part of the above definition, known as the "transmit clause," is the focus of the courts' legal analysis in the *Aereo* and *FilmOn* cases.

Transmit Clause

Congress added the "Transmit Clause" during the 1976 revisions of the previous copyright laws in order to accommodate developing technologies. The transmit clause identifies four elements that trigger a public performance: (1) a transmission or other communication, (2) of a performance of the work, (3) to members of the public who are capable of receiving the performance, and (4) where the transmission either is to a public or semi-public place, or is to members of the public who may be separated geographically or temporally or both.[20]

Transmission or Other Communication

The first element incorporates the Copyright Act's definition of "transmit." Under the Copyright Act, a transmission of a performance or display is a "communicat[ion] by any device or process whereby images or sounds are received beyond the place from which they are sent."[21] Congress intended this broad definition "to include all conceivable forms and combination of wired or wireless communications media, including but by no means limited to radio and television broadcasting as we know them."[22] Similarly, the U.S. Court of Appeals for the Ninth Circuit, in *Columbia Pictures Industries, Inc. v. Professional Real Estate Investors, Inc.*, held that to transmit a public performance "at least involves sending out some sort of signal via a device or process to be received by the public at a place beyond the place from which it is sent."[23]

Performance of the Work

The second element requires the transmission to involve a performance of the work. The Copyright Act defines "to perform" as "to recite, render, play, dance, or act it, either directly or by means of any device or process or, in the case of a motion picture or other audiovisual work, to show its images in any sequences or to make the sounds accompanying it audible."[24]

For certain mediums, such as literary works, courts distinguish between the transmission of the work itself and the transmission of a performance or recitation of the work.[25] However, such a distinction does not reasonably apply to audiovisual works. For example, television broadcasts may be characterized as performances transmitted by the studio of another performance of an underlying work (that particular television show).[26] In this context, courts may need to consider whether the broadcast or a retransmission of that broadcast is a separate performance itself compared to the performance of the underlying work.

Members of the Public Capable of Receiving the Performance

The third element addresses the basic nature of the public performance right. While the Copyright Act does not explicitly define "public," the definition of a "public performance" indicates that "public" includes spaces accessible to the public or places outside of the normal gatherings of the family.[27] However, courts have interpreted "public" to include a broader range of people in places that traditionally are considered nonpublic. The U.S. District Court for the Northern District of California held *in On Command Video Corp. v. Columbia Pictures Industries* that transmitting a video rental to a guest in his hotel room constituted a transmission of a public performance because of the commercial nature of the rental even though the viewing itself occurred in a "nonpublic" place.[28]

Courts have relied upon the phrase "capable of receiving the performance" as the primary qualifier for determining whether a potential recipient is public or private. Interpretation of this phrase has been the primary issue in the cases leading up to the *Aereo* and *FilmOn* decisions. In *Cartoon Network LP v. CSC Holdings, Inc. (*"Cablevision")[29], the Second Circuit stated that "capable of receiving the performance" means "capable of receiving a particular transmission of a performance" because the transmission is itself a performance.[30] This case involved a remote storage digital video recorder (RS-DVR) service that streamed a unique playback copy of a television program stored on a subscriber's individual hard drive.[31] The Second Circuit held that because the "RS-DVR playback transmission is made to a single subscriber using a single unique copy produced by that subscriber" the playback transmissions were not public performances and, therefore, did not infringe upon the plaintiffs' exclusive right of public performance.[32] According to the court, this element of the "transmit clause" requires consideration of the potential audience of a particular *transmission* and not of the underlying work, as the potential audience for any copyrighted work is the general public. Cablevision's RS-DVR system enabled each subscriber to access that particular playback copy available only to that particular subscriber.[33]

Separated Geographically or Temporally

The development of technology triggered the last element: transmission either is to a public or semi-public place, or is to members of the public who may be separated geographically or temporally or both. Because of greater accessibility generated by developing technologies, a performance no longer needs to occur in a single place such as a theater but can often occur in a more private place such as a home or a car.

However, receiving a transmission at different times and/or different places does not diminish the public nature of the performance. In *Columbia Pictures Industries, Inc. v. Redd Horne, Inc.,* a video store transmitted at different times the same copy of a film to multiple customers, who each viewed the film in a private room in the store.[34] The U.S. Court of Appeals for the Third Circuit held that these transmissions were public performances. Even though the customers viewed the film in traditionally private rooms at different times, the transmission of the single copy of the film still served as a public performance.[35]

AEREO'S INTERPRETATION OF THE TRANSMIT CLAUSE

In 2012, a group of broadcasters filed copyright infringement actions against Aereo in the U.S. District Court for the Southern District of New York. In *American Broadcasting Companies v. Aereo,* the district court denied the plaintiffs' motion for a preliminary injunction barring Aereo from transmitting television programs.[36] In *WNET v. Aereo,* the plaintiffs appealed the district court's denial to the U.S. Court of Appeals for the Second Circuit.[37] On April 1, 2013, the Second Circuit affirmed the district court's ruling that refused to grant the injunction against Aereo. The court held that Aereo's transmissions of broadcast television programs were not public performances under the Copyright Act because the transmissions are of unique copies created at the user's request.[38] The following discussion will examine the Second Circuit's interpretation of the transmit clause in reaching this decision. The court focused on two out of the four elements of the transmit clause discussed above: "performance of the work" and "members of the public capable of receiving the performance." These factors contribute to the alleged "loophole" used by Aereo's one-antenna-per-subscriber service to avoid infringing the public performance right.

Performance of the Work

The Copyright Act defines "performance"[39] as specific actions such as reciting, rendering, playing, or showing of images. However, for broadcasts and retransmissions, courts must determine which "performance" is at issue when considering whether the transmission violated the copyright holder's public performance right.

The specific issue before the Second Circuit in *Aereo* was what performance triggers the analysis in the Copyright Act's transmit clause: the broadcast of the program or the specific transmission created by Aereo. The plaintiffs in *Aereo* argued that the court should consider each of Aereo's transmissions in the aggregate in order to determine whether they are public performances because the transmissions are of the same underlying program watched by many members of the public.[40]

The Second Circuit dismissed this interpretation, stating that the plaintiffs' argument misreads the transmit clause. For the Second Circuit, the performance at issue was the particular transmission created by the Aereo system for that specific user.[41] Each of Aereo's transmissions was an independent performance because each transmission is a unique copy by Aereo's system.[42] These transmissions were not equal to the original broadcast performance. Equating them as such, according to the court, would disregard the transmit clause's specific inquiry regarding a particular transmission. In reaching this conclusion, the Second Circuit relied upon its previous decision in *Cablevision*, which held that individual copies made by an RS-DVR system were the performances at issue.[43]

Members of the Public Capable of Receiving the Performance

This analysis led to the Second Circuit's next point concerning the transmit clause and the composition of the audience to trigger a public performance. Similar to their argument concerning performance, the plaintiffs argued that "members of the public" includes the potential audience for the broadcast and not the individual transmission.[44] According to the court, however, the relevant inquiry under the transmit clause concerning the definition of "public" is "the potential audience of a particular transmission, not the potential audience for the underlying work or the particular performance of that work being transmitted."[45] The Second Circuit supported this interpretation of the transmit clause by stating that the potential audience for the underlying work could include anyone, making the differentiation between public and nonpublic performances irrelevant.[46]

Reiterating a similar argument in *Cablevision*, the court referred to the presence of "to the public" in the transmit clause to support the supposition that not all transmissions are automatically public performances.[47] The court further acknowledged that Aereo has designed its retransmission system to accommodate this distinction in the Copyright Act. Each user has a specific antenna transmitting a specific copy of the program only to that user.[48] When an Aereo subscriber selects to watch or record a program, Aereo's system creates a unique copy of that program that is accessible on the hard drive only by that subscriber. Therefore, the Second Circuit concluded that the potential audience of that particular transmission is only one subscriber who is capable of receiving that particular transmission/performance.[49]

Dissent

The dissent in *WNET v. Aereo* focused on criticizing the majority's understanding and analysis of the transmit clause. First, the dissent stated that Aereo's transmissions are public performances within the plain meaning of the statute. Using a dictionary definition of "public," the dissent maintained that anything not transmitted to oneself is a communication to a member of the public and, therefore, Aereo is engaging in a public performance for each of its transmissions.[50]

The dissent also referred to the legislative history of the transmit clause to show that Congress anticipated developing technology such as Aereo's system. For the dissent, the addition of the "different times/places" phrasing to the transmit clause demonstrated Congressional intent that the public performance right encompass a broad scope.[51] Specifically, for the dissent, the House Report's explanation that "if the transmission reaches the public in [any] form" the transmission comes within the scope of the public performance right verified his interpretation.[52]

The dissent also found Aereo's system distinct from the RS-DVR technology at issue in *Cablevision*.[53] Cablevision's RS-DVR system produced copies of material that Cablevision already had a license to retransmit while Aereo's system enables it to transmit material to subscribers without a license. Thus, according to the dissent, the *Cablevision* analysis of the transmit clause should not even apply to Aereo.[54]

FILMON X'S INTERPRETATION OF THE TRANSMIT CLAUSE

In the 2012 case *Fox Television Stations, Inc. v. BarryDriller Content Systems PLC,* the plaintiffs, several broadcast television networks, brought an action against FilmOn in the U.S. District Court for the Central District of California.[55] The plaintiffs alleged that FilmOn's retransmission of their broadcasts infringed their copyright, specifically the right of public performance. Unlike in *Aereo*, the district court granted a partial injunction against the defendant from offering its content in that particular area of the country.[56]

A year later, the same plaintiffs brought another suit against FilmOn in the U.S. District Court for the District of Columbia, in *Fox Television Stations, Inc. v. FilmOn X LLC,* alleging the same violation of rights.[57] While FilmOn's arguments relied upon the *Aereo* decision in the Second Circuit, the district court granted the injunction for the plaintiffs, citing FilmOn's violation of the plaintiffs' public performance right of their copyrighted works.[58]

In both cases, the courts found that the retransmissions of broadcast content over the Internet were public performances and therefore infringed the plaintiffs' exclusive rights. The following sections will examine the district courts' interpretation of the transmit clause and why they found violations of the transmit clause in these cases, despite the similarities in technology with Aereo.[59] Again the courts' analysis focused on the same two elements of the transmit clause: "performance of the work" and "members of the public capable of receiving the performance."

Performance of the Work

Both the D.C. and California district courts emphasized the scope of "performance" in the transmit clause in finding that FilmOn violated the plaintiffs' right to public performance. For the California district court in *BarryDriller,* the performance that triggers the transmit clause is that of the copyrighted work itself and not the retransmission of its performance.[60] According to the California district court, the Copyright Act does not justify the Second Circuit's focus in *Aereo* on the uniqueness of the individual copy from which the transmission is made.[61] Instead, the court stated that the

Copyright Act directs the court to look at the performance of the underlying copyrighted work.

The D.C. district court further clarified in its opinion that "performance" refers to a communication of the original over-the-air broadcast of a copyrighted work and not just the retransmission itself.[62] The court cited legislative history of the Copyright Act, specifically the House Report's explanation of "public performance."[63] According to the Report, Congress intended "public performance" to include "not only the initial rendition or showing, but also any further act by which that rendition or showing is transmitted or communicated to the public," supporting the court's broad interpretation of "performance."[64]

Members of the Public Capable of Receiving the Performance

In addition to defining the scope of "performance" in the transmit clause, the D.C. district court considered the definition of "public," dismissing the Second Circuit's interpretation. For the D.C. district court, "public" in the transmit clause includes "any member of the public who accesses the FilmOn service."[65] The court stated that the determination of whether an audience is public should not depend on technological access and development, including how television signals are transmitted and received. The Second Circuit's emphasis of the one-antenna per subscriber aspect of the system in *Aereo* ignored, according to the D.C. district court, the single tuner server, router, and encoder that communicate with all of the antennas.[66] Additionally, the D.C. district court found that Congress did not intend the development of new technologies to circumvent the public aspect of the transmit clause when it enacted this provision to include communication "by any device or process."[67] Moreover, because the relationship between FilmOn and the subscribers was commercial, the court reasoned that the transmission/performance is public regardless of where or how the consumption takes place.

FUTURE LITIGATION

The contrasting outcomes of these lawsuits demonstrate two different interpretations of the transmit clause in the Copyright Act, specifically the meaning of "performance" and "members of the public capable of receiving the performance." The Second Circuit in the *Aereo* cases interpreted "performance" in the transmit clause as the specific transmission created by Aereo for that user and not the transmission of the underlying work. For the Second Circuit, if the transmission of the underlying work triggered the public performance right, then every performance would be public and not private. However, the D.C. and California district courts dismissed this reasoning and used legislative history to interpret "performance" to mean that of the underlying work.

Likewise, the courts disagreed as to the scope of "members of the public capable of receiving the performance." Similar to its reasoning regarding "performance," the Second Circuit held that "members of the public" includes only those capable of receiving the particular transmission copy created by Aereo. Because each subscriber receives a unique copy, the transmission is not a public performance. The D.C. district court, however, did not use technological access to define "members of the public" but looked at the potential audience for the service. The D.C. district court supported this interpretation by stating that Congress did not intend the development of technology, including this method of Internet television streaming, to bypass copyright protections.

These different interpretations foreshadow further litigation on this subject and possible issues for appeal. The Second Circuit in *WNET v. Aereo* acknowledged that its decision that Aereo's service is a private transmission was prompted primarily by stare decisis and the earlier holding in *Cablevision*. The court emphasized that it is "bound by the decisions of prior panels until such time as they are overruled either by an en banc panel of our Court or by the Supreme Court."[68] Here, the court has acknowledged the prospect of future litigation.[69] However, the Second Circuit denied the plaintiffs' petition for rehearing en banc.[70]

In January 2014, the U.S. Supreme Court granted a petition for writ of certiorari filed by the plaintiffs (petitioners) in *WNET v. Aereo*.[71] In the petition, the petitioners argued that the Second Circuit decision, *WNET v. Aereo*, is "a fundamentally flawed reading of the Transmit Clause."[72] According to the petitioners, the transmit clause requires the inquiry to focus on whether the public "is capable of receiving the *performance*" and not "whether it is capable of receiving the *transmission*" as interpreted by the Second Circuit.[73] The petitioners also argued that the Second Circuit decision raises questions as to the viability of the current broadcast programming model and harms the broadcast television industry, specifically restricting their ability "to control how their programming is used by others."[74] In its answer, Aereo reiterated the arguments made in *WNET v. Aereo* that its transmissions are not public performances because each transmission is a "unique copy of a performance of a work, created at the direction of the user, [and] is transmitted only by and to that user."[75] Aereo also argued that the Copyright Act distinguishes between those "capable of receiving" a transmission and actually "receiving it" to support their conclusion that the unique copy received only by a specific user is a private performance.[76]

The Supreme Court has denied FilmOn's motion to intervene in support of Aereo.[77] Several entertainment industry groups and legal copyright practitioners have filed amicus briefs in favor of the broadcasters. The National Football League and Major League Baseball have stated in their brief that they would consider moving major league sports broadcasts away from the public airwaves and place them exclusively on cable to avoid "hijacking" by Aereo-like services.[78] The brief filed by the Screen Actors Guild declared that Congress specifically adopted the transmit clause to capture secondary transmissions of primary transmissions like Aereo's retransmissions of broadcasts and argued that widespread implementation of such a service would harm the entertainment industry.[79] The U.S. government also filed a brief in support of the broadcasters, in which it argued that Aereo's transmissions fall within the Copyright Act's public performance definition.[80]

FilmOn has filed an appeal with the U.S. Court of Appeals for the District of Columbia Circuit to lift the injunction issued by the D.C. district court in *Fox Television Stations v. FilmOn X.*[81] FilmOn has argued that the near-nationwide injunction set by the D.C. district court places the company at an "unfair competitive disadvantage" with Aereo, which is expanding its service throughout the country.[82]

RELATED LEGISLATION IN THE 113TH CONGRESS

In its analysis of *WNET v. Aereo,* the Second Circuit alluded to the opportunity for congressional action. Specifically, the court discussed differences in technology in 1976 and 2013 and the resulting difficulty in distinguishing between private and public transmissions.[83] In deciding that Aereo's service is a private transmission, the court concluded that "unanticipated technological developments have created tension between Congress's view that retransmissions of network programs by cable television systems should be deemed public performances and its intent that some transmissions be classified as private."[84] By emphasizing this conflict between the law and developing technology, the court has highlighted an opportunity for congressional action and clarification of the Copyright Act.[85]

Several bills introduced during the 113th Congress would implicate the various parties in the *Aereo* and *FilmOn* cases. The Television Consumer Freedom Act of 2013,[86] introduced by Senator John McCain, would impact the market in which companies such as Aereo, FilmOn, and the broadcasters are competing. The act would allow cable providers to offer to subscribers "a la carte" programming: programming on a per-channel basis rather than as part of a package.[87] The bill would also deny broadcasters their spectrum licenses if they moved big event programming from broadcast television to cable.[88] Many of the *Aereo* plaintiffs have threatened this action in response to Aereo's success in the courts.[89]

The Consumer Choice in Online Video Act,[90] introduced by Senator Jay Rockefeller, seeks to increase consumer choice and competition in the online video programming marketplace. The bill would prohibit content distributors from engaging in unfair or deceptive practices.[91] The bill also contains provisions that would address antenna rental services, such as Aereo, specifically. These provisions would exempt these services from paying certain retransmission fees.[92] However, these provisions assume that the online video provider is legally operating and obtaining content, stressing the need for further clarification from the courts concerning the legal status of companies such as Aereo and FilmOn X.

End Notes

[1] See, e.g., Jeff Bercovici, How Amazon and Netflix Are, and Aren't, Changing TV, FORBES, November 14, 2013, http://www.forbes.com/sites/jeffbercovici/2013/11/04/how-amazon-and-netflix-are-and-arent-changing-tv/.

[2] See George Winslow, Diller: Aereo Is 'Not a Loophole; It is a Right,' BROADCASTING & CABLE, April 29, 2013, http://www.broadcastingcable.com/news/technology/diller-aereo-not-loophole-it-right/49951.

[3] 17 U.S.C. §106.

[4] ABC v. Aereo, 874 F.Supp. 2d 373 (S.D.N.Y. 2012).

[5] Fox Television Stations, Inc. v. BarryDriller Content Systems PLC, 915 F. Supp.2d 1138 (C.D. Cal. 2013).

[6] Fox Televisions Stations Inc. v. FilmOn X LLC, No. 13-758 (D.D.C. 2013).

[7] FilmOn X, No. 13-758 at FN 4. The differences between FilmOn and Aereo systems are "minor distinctions in the sequence in which signals are processed." However, "the systems are essentially the same, and the parties agree that there are no legally meaningful differences."

[8] ABC, 874 F.Supp. 2d at 377. For more information about DVR technology, see CRS Report RL34719, Cartoon Network LP v. CSC Holdings, Inc.: Remote-Storage Digital Video Recorders and Copyright Law, by Kate M. Manuel.

[9] The Future of TV: How Do Networks Plan to Stay Competitive? PBS NEWSHOUR, September 25, 2013, http://www.pbs.org/newshour/bb/media/july-dec13/comcast_09-25.html.

[10] WNET v. Aereo, 712 F.3d 676, 681-82 (2d Cir. 2013).

[11] Id. at 682.

[12] Id.

[13] FilmOn X, No. 13-758 at *5.

[14] WNET, 712 F.3d at 682.

[15] Id.

[16] Id. at 683.

[17] 17 U.S.C. §106.

[18] 17 U.S.C. §106(4).

[19] 17 U.S.C. §101.

[20] 17 U.S.C. §101.

[21] Id.

[22] H.Rept. 94-1476, at 64.

[23] Columbia Pictures Industries, Inc. v. Professional Real Estate Investors, Inc., 866 F.2d 278, 282 (9th Cir. 1989).

[24] 17 U.S.C. §101.

[25] Kent D. Stuckey, INTERNET AND ONLINE LAW, §6.08(4).

[26] Id.

[27] See 17 U.S.C. §101.

[28] On Command Video Corp. v. Columbia Pictures Industries, 777 F.Supp. 787, 790 (N.D. Cal. 1991).

[29] See CRS Report RL34719, Cartoon Network LP v. CSC Holdings, Inc.: Remote-Storage Digital Video Recorders and Copyright Law, by Kate M. Manuel.

[30] Cartoon Network LP v. CSC Holdings, Inc. ("Cablevision"), 536 F.3d 121, 134-35 (2d Cir. 2008).

[31] See CRS Report RL34719, Cartoon Network LP v. CSC Holdings, Inc.: Remote-Storage Digital Video Recorders and Copyright Law, by Kate M. Manuel for a discussion about RS-DVR playback transmissions.

[32] Cablevision, 536 F.3d at 139.

[33] Id. at 136.

[34] Columbia Pictures Industries, Inc. v. Redd Horne, Inc., 749 F.2d 154 (3d Cir. 1984).

[35] Id. at 159.

[36] ABC, 874 F.Supp. 2d at 375.

[37] WNET, 712 F.3d at 680. The case name is different on appeal because two groups of plaintiffs initially filed separate copyright infringement actions against Aereo. They later proceeded before the district court in tandem before together seeking the appeal.

[38] WNET, 712 F.3d at 696.

[39] 17 U.S.C. §101.

[40] WNET, 712 F.3d at 690-91.

[41] Id. at 691.

[42] Id. at 690.

[43] WNET, 712 F.3d at 689-90.

[44] See id. at 690.
[45] Id. at 691.
[46] Id.
[47] Id. at 694. The Second Circuit in Cablevision argued that because only one person could access the specific copy made by the RS-DVR, the potential audience for that particular performance consisted of that single person.
[48] Id. at 693-94.
[49] Id. at 690.
[50] Id. at 698.
[51] WNET, 712 F.3d at 700.
[52] WNET, 712 F.3d at 701 (citing H. Rept. 94-1476, at 64).
[53] WNET, 712 F.3d at 701-02.
[54] Id. at 703.
[55] BarryDriller, 915 F. Supp.2d at 1140.
[56] Id. at 1148.
[57] FilmOn X, No. 13-758 at *1.
[58] Id. The geographic scope of the injunction is limited to the Ninth Circuit.
[59] The D.C. and California district courts are not bound by the decision issued in the Second Circuit because they are located in different circuits.
[60] BarryDriller, 915 F. Supp.2d at 1144.
[61] Id. at 1144-46.
[62] FilmOn X., No. 13-758 at *26-28.
[63] Id. at *26.
[64] FilmOn X., No. 13-758 at *26 (citing H.Rept. 94-1476, at 5676-77).
[65] FilmOn X., No. 13-758 at *25.
[66] Id. at *26-27.
[67] Id. at *27.
[68] WNET, 712 F.3d at 695 (citing U.S. v. Wilkerson, 361 F.3d 717, 732 (2d Cir. 2004)).
[69] Barry Werbin, WNET v. Aereo, THE ENTERTAINMENT, ARTS AND SPORTS LAW BLOG (April 1, 2013 1:110 PM), (http://nysbar.com/blogs/EASL/2013/04/wnet_v_aereo.html).
[70] WNET v. Aereo, 722 F.3d 500 (2d Cir. 2013).
[71] Docket for 13-461 ABC v. Aereo, http://www.supremecourt.gov/Search.aspx?FileName=/docketfiles/13-461.htm.
[72] Petition for Writ of Certiorari, ABC v. Aereo, No. 13-461 at 25, http://sblog.s3.amazonaws.com/wp-content/uploads/ 2013/11/ABCvAereo_11Oct13.pdf.
[73] Id. at 26 (emphasis in original).
[74] Id. at 32, 34.
[75] Response to Petition for Writ of Certiorari, ABC v. Aereo, No. 13-461 at 14 http://sblog.s3.amazonaws.com/wpcontent/uploads/2013/12/13-461-Aereo-response-brief.pdf.
[76] Id. at 15.
[77] Docket for 13-461 ABC v. Aereo, http://www.supremecourt.gov/Search.aspx? FileName=/docketfiles/13-461.htm.
[78] Brief for National Football League and Major League Baseball as Amici Curiae Supporting Petitioners, ABC v. Aereo, (No. 13-461), at 23.
[79] Brief for Screen Actors Guild-American Federation of Television and Radio Artists, et al. as Amici Curiae Supporting Petitioners, ABC v. Aereo, (No. 13-461), at 19, 32.

[80] Brief for the United States as Amicus Curiae Supporting Petitioners, ABC v. Aereo, (No. 13-461), at 12.

[81] Wendy Davis, FilmOn X Asks Appeals Court to Lift Ban, ONLINE MEDIA DAILY, December 6, 2013, http://www.mediapost.com/publications/article/214993/filmon-x-asks-appeals-court-to-lift-ban.html.

[82] Id.

[83] WNET, 712 F.3d at 695.

[84] Id. at 695.

[85] For further discussion on the current statutory framework for online distributors, see CRS Report R42722, Online Video Distributors and the Current Statutory and Regulatory Framework: Issues for Congress, by Charles B. Goldfarb, Kathleen Ann Ruane, and Patricia Moloney Figliola and CRS Report R43248, Updating the Statutory Framework for Communications for the Digital Age: Issues for Congress, by Charles B. Goldfarb and Patricia Moloney Figliola.

[86] S. 912.

[87] S. 912, §3.

[88] S. 912, §4.

[89] See Joe Flint, John McCain introduces Television Consumer Freedom Act of 2013, L.A. TIMES, MAY 9, 2013, http://www.latimes.com/entertainment/envelope/cotown/la-et-ct-mccain-cable20130509,0,2224732.story#axzz2nIMEmfk9.

[90] S. 1680.

[91] S. 1680, §201.

[92] Id.

In: Internet Television Streaming …
Editor: Meredith Lane

ISBN: 978-1-63321-723-2

Chapter 2

CARTOON NETWORK LP V. CSC HOLDINGS, INC.: REMOTE-STORAGE DIGITAL VIDEO RECORDERS AND COPYRIGHT LAW*

Kate M. Manuel

SUMMARY

The time-shifting technologies that consumers use to record television programs as they are broadcast and to play them back later have long prompted allegations of copyright infringement from broadcast networks and movie studios. However, as the technologies have evolved and lawsuits against their manufacturers have been resolved, the nature of the copyright claims has changed. In 2006, broadcasters and studios sued Cablevision over its proposed remote-storage digital video recording service, which would allow consumers to record and play back broadcast content using Cablevision's facilities instead of in-home devices. Because the recordings were made at Cablevision's facilities and the playbacks were transmitted from there, content owners claimed direct infringement of their reproduction and public performance rights. Previously, copyright holders had claimed contributory or vicarious infringement by manufacturers of recording devices.

* This is an edited, reformatted and augmented version of a Congressional Research Service publication RL34719, prepared for Members and Committees of Congress, dated July 6, 2009.

In 2007, a federal district court in New York found for the plaintiffs and enjoined Cablevision from operating its proposed recording service, holding that (1) the unauthorized buffer and playback copies made when recording broadcast programming were infringing reproductions, and (2) the unauthorized transmissions of playback copies to consumers were infringing public performances.

In 2008, the U.S. Court of Appeals for the Second Circuit reversed the district court. It found that neither buffer nor playback copies infringed content owners' reproduction rights. According to the appellate court, the buffer copies were non-infringing because they were embodied too briefly for fixation to occur and to count as "copies" under the Copyright Act. The playback copies were similarly non-infringing because Cablevision's customers, not Cablevision, created them. Additionally, the Second Circuit found that Cablevision's transmission of playback copies to consumers did not infringe content owners' public performance rights. The transmissions were non-infringing because Cablevision made individualized copies of every television show for each recording customer and customers could view only "their" copies.

Beyond clarifying the nature of infringing reproductions and public performances under the Copyright Act, the Second Circuit's *Cartoon Network* decision, coupled with the Supreme Court's subsequent denial of certiorari in the case, paves the way for Cablevision to market the first-ever remote-storage digital video recording service. This effect of the *Cartoon Network* decision could potentially be undercut by the parties' failure to allege contributory infringement, vicarious infringement, or fair use, as well as by the fact that the decision is binding precedent only within the Second Circuit. However, to the degree that courts in other circuits follow the Second Circuit, they may view remote-storage digital video recorders as successors to video cassette recorders and set-top-storage digital video recorders, protecting manufacturers of the latest time-shifting technologies from liability for copyright infringement.

In *Cartoon Network LP v. CSC Holdings, Inc.*, a three-judge panel of the U.S. Court of Appeals for the Second Circuit held that Cablevision's proposed remote-storage digital video recording (RS-DVR) service did not directly infringe the reproduction or public performance rights of those holding copyrights in the recorded materials.[1] Under the Copyright Act of 1976, copyright holders have exclusive rights to reproduce their works in copies and to perform motion pictures or other audiovisual works publicly.[2] Network broadcasters, cable broadcasters, and movie studios argued that Cablevision's proposed service would infringe these rights by creating unauthorized, unlicensed, and therefore infringing buffer and playback copies of their programs and transmitting the playback copies to customers.[3] Although the U.S. District Court for the Southern District of New York agreed with the copyright holders and permanently enjoined Cablevision from operating its RS-DVR service on March 22, 2007,[4] the Second Circuit reversed on August 4, 2008. The Second Circuit's decision clarifies the nature of infringing reproduction and public performance under the Copyright Act and, coupled with the Supreme Court's subsequent denial of certiorari in the case, paves the way for commercial introduction of the latest technology for time-shifted viewing of television programming.

TIME-SHIFTING TECHNOLOGIES AND LITIGATION

RS-DVR is the latest technology enabling consumers to "time shift" televison programming by recording content at the time it is broadcast for future viewing. Video cassette recorders (VCRs) and set-top storage DVRs (STS-DVRs) offer similar capabilities. However, each of these technologies operates differently and has been subject to differing allegations of copyright infringement. Because the various time-shifting technologies and the cases resolving copyright claims against them underlie the *Cartoon Network* decision, they are briefly reviewed here.

VCRs and the *Sony* Decision

A VCR is a device that consumers connect to their television sets in order to record audio and video content onto magnetic tape for future playback.[5] When Sony began selling its Betamax VCR in the 1970s, Universal Studios and Walt Disney sued Sony for contributory copyright infringement.[6] Universal and Disney had licensed broadcasters to transmit their copyrighted programs to the public, but had not authorized or licensed Sony or members of the general public to make copies of them.[7] Universal and Disney worried that consumers' unauthorized, unlicensed copying could harm them by diminishing the audience for original broadcasts and thereby decreasing ratings and advertising rates.[8]

In their lawsuit against Sony, Universal and Disney argued (1) that consumers infringed the companies' exclusive rights to reproduce their programming by recording TV programs with the Betamax VCR and (2) that Sony should be liable for consumers' infringement because it made the

Betamax available to consumers.[9] The U.S. Supreme Court disagreed, however. The Court first found that consumer recording of broadcast television was a non-infringing fair use because consumer time-shifting of television viewing did not demonstrably harm content owners, whose shows were still watched, albeit at different times than their scheduled broadcast times.[10] The Court further found that Sony was not liable for contributory infringement merely for manufacturing or selling the Betamax because "the sale of copying equipment ... does not constitute contributory infringement if the product is widely used for legitimate, unobjectionable purposes."[11]

STS-DVRs and the *ReplayTV* Litigation

In the early 2000s, STS-DVRs began to replace VCRs. STS-DVRs resemble VCRs in that they are devices that consumers purchase from manufacturers, install in their homes, connect to their televisions, and use to record broadcasts for later viewing. Their main difference from VCRs is that they record broadcasts in digital rather than analog format.[12] Digital recording brought two other changes that concerned content owners, though. Digital recording and replay devices can be programmed to automatically skip television commercials.[13] They can also make and distribute perfect digital copies of broadcast content.[14] Both these features of STS-DVRs suggested, at least to broadcasters and movie studios, that the harm caused by unauthorized, unlicensed consumer recording with STS-DVRs was greater than that with VCRs. Thus, when broadcasters and movie studios sued early STS-DVR manufacturers ReplayTV and SonicBlue alleging contributory and vicarious copyright infringement, they hoped for different judicial findings on (1) whether consumers' time-shifting recordings were infringing and (2) whether the manufacturers of consumers' recording devices were liable for consumers' conduct.[15] Consumers intervened in the case to establish that their use of STS-DVRs was non-infringing,[16] and the parties eventually settled without a judicial decision addressing whether STS-DVRs, like their VCR predecessors, are non-infringing time-shifting technologies.[17]

Cablevision's RS-DVRs

In 2006, Cablevision, a telecommunications and entertainment company, announced plans to add RS-DVR service to the array of high-speed Internet, digital cable TV, and digital telephone services that it offers to consumers.[18] RS-DVRs differ from traditional STS-DVRs because consumers do not need to install devices or wiring in their homes to record or store broadcast content. They need only a remote control and a set-top receiver to select programming for recording and to play it back. All recordings are made and stored using the facilities of the RSDVR provider, a technical development that analysts projected could double the market for DVRs.[19]

Cablevision's RS-DVR service, in particular, is designed so that each user creates and views separate copies of each television program that Cablevision broadcasts.[20] Cablevision takes the stream of data—digitally representing the broadcast content—and splits it into two streams as "live" transmission begins.[21] The first stream is transmitted to Cablevision subscribers in real time, as the show airs.[22] The second stream is sent to a buffer, or an area of computer memory used to store data temporarily. The buffer retains up to 1.2 seconds of each program at a time while Cablevision's computers determine whether any customers requested recording of the program.[23] If a customer requested recording, the second stream is sent to a second buffer, from which the program is copied to the customer's hard-drive storage space on Cablevision's computers for future playback.[24] The customer can request that this recording be transmitted for viewing at any time after the program's broadcast begins.[25]

Cablevision had licenses with the broadcasters and networks allowing it to transmit their copyrighted programming to consumers "live."[26] It did not have licenses to make buffer or playback copies, or to transmit playback copies to consumers.

Corporations owning copyrights in broadcast content argued that Cablevision's RS-DVR service would infringe their reproduction and public performance rights by making unauthorized and unlicensed buffer and playback copies of television programs and by engaging in unauthorized and unlicensed transmission of playback copies to customers.[27] They sued to enjoin Cablevision's operation of its RS-DVR service.[28] Although Cablevision's customers were engaging in an activity—time-shifted viewing of broadcast television—protected under *Sony*, the technologies and legal claims involved differed from those in earlier VCR and STS-DVR cases. Cablevision did not sell devices to consumers that they used to copy and play back broadcast content in their homes; rather, it used its facilities to record, store, and transmit playback copies for consumers. Additionally, the Cablevision plaintiffs alleged direct copyright infringement, or unlawful activity by Cablevision itself, not contributory or vicarious infringement, as in *Sony* and *Paramount*.[29] Cablevision further agreed not to assert a fair-use defense in the litigation.[30]

Table 1. Comparison of Time-Shifting Technologies

Technology	Distinguishing Features	Allegations of Infringement	Outcome of Litigation
VCR	* Set-top boxes purchased from manufacturers, installed and operated in-home * Analog copies	* Contributory infringement of the reproduction right, alleged against VCR manufacturer	* Supreme Court held that time-shifting consumer recording with a VCR is non-infringing * Supreme Court held that the manufacturer is not liable for devices with substantial non-infringing uses
STS-DVR	* Set-top boxes purchased from manufacturers, installed and operated in home * Digital copies	* Contributory infringement of the reproduction and distribution rights, alleged against STS-DVR manufacturer * Vicarious infringement of the reproduction and distribution rights, alleged against STS-DVR manufacturer	* Ninth Circuit dismissed without judgment on the merits
Cablevision's RS-DVR	* Consumers record and save broadcast programming on Cablevision's equipment * Digital copies	* Direct infringement of the reproduction and public performance rights, alleged against RS-DVR manufacturer	* Second Circuit held that buffer copies lasting 1.2 seconds do not infringe the reproduction right * Second Circuit held that customers make the playback copies with RS-DVRs * Second Circuit held that transmission of playback copies does not infringe the public performance right

Source: Congressional Research Service.

THE CARTOON NETWORK HOLDINGS

The district court in the *Cartoon Network* case sided with the copyright holders, finding that unauthorized buffer and playback copies were infringing reproductions and that unauthorized transmissions of playback copies to RS-DVR customers were infringing public performances.[31] The circuit court disagreed, however, because of its interpretation of the nature of infringing reproductions and public performances under the Copyright Act.[32]

Reproduction under the Copyright Act: The Meaning of "Fixation" and "Copies"

The Copyright Act grants copyright owners the exclusive right "to reproduce the copyrighted work in copies."[33] The word "reproduce" is not defined within the act, but the word "copies" is.[34] Copies are "material objects, other than phonorecords, in which a work is fixed by any method now known or later developed, and from which the work can be perceived, reproduced, or otherwise communicated, either directly or with the aid of a machine or device."[35] The act further defines the term "fixed," used within the definition of "copies," as follows:

> A work is "fixed" in a tangible medium of expression when its embodiment in a copy or phonorecord, by or under the authority of the author, is sufficiently permanent or stable to permit it to be perceived, reproduced, or otherwise communicated for a period of more than transitory duration. A work consisting of sounds, images, or both, that are being transmitted, is "fixed" for purposes of this title if a fixation of the work is being made simultaneously with its transmission.[36]

The meanings of "embodiment" and "for a period of more than transitory duration" are not specified within the act but are key to the definition of "fixation."[37] In short, fixation requires embodiment for a more-than-transitory duration, and without fixation, there cannot be "copies" under the Copyright Act or infringing reproduction.

The first claim of the *Cartoon Network* plaintiffs was that Cablevision infringed their copyrights by reproducing their programs when making unauthorized, unlicensed buffer copies prior to recording content for Cablevision customers.[38] Embodiment was not at issue, given the facts of the case, because "every second of an entire work [was] placed, one second at a time, in the buffer," from which it was copied.[39] Whether the embodiment was for a period of more than transitory duration was disputed, however.[40] Both the plaintiffs and the district court, which found for the plaintiffs, relied upon case law suggesting that embodiment *per se* suffices for fixation.[41] The plaintiffs and the district court further relied upon a report from the U.S. Copyright Office stating that any duration requirement for fixation is met "[u]nless a reproduction manifests itself so fleetingly that *it cannot be copied*."[42] Cablevision, in contrast, argued that its buffer copies did not constitute "copies" under the Copyright Act because they were not fixed and thus were not embodied for a sufficient time.[43] Cablevision emphasized that its buffer copies existed for "no ... more than 1.2 seconds before being automatically overwritten."[44] Cablevision further argued that even assuming fixation, any "copies" were "otherwise de minimis" because they involved no more than 1.2 seconds of broadcast content.[45]

The Second Circuit found for Cablevision, holding that embodiment in a buffer for 1.2 seconds fails to qualify as embodiment for a more-than-transitory duration.[46] According to the Second Circuit, because embodiment was not for a more-than-transitory duration, no fixation occurred; no "copies" were made under the Copyright Act; and Cablevision engaged in no infringing reproduction with its buffer copies.[47]

The Second Circuit thus gave its answer to a question long discussed by copyright scholars: how long must a work be embodied for fixation to occur?[48] However, its answer may diverge from that of other federal circuits, some of which have indicated that copies existing in random access memory (RAM) for seconds or minutes are fixed and thus meet any duration requirement for embodiment.[49] In *MAI Systems Corporation v. Peak Computer, Inc.*, for example, the Ninth Circuit found that a computer company created a "copy," for purposes of the Copyright Act, when its employee loaded copyrighted software into RAM for a very brief time in order to view system error logs and diagnose problems while repairing a computer.[50] The Second Circuit attempted to distinguish cases such as *MAI Systems* by noting that copies in RAM often exist for minutes as opposed to seconds and by reading prior cases to say that loading content into RAM may—but does not necessarily—result in infringing reproduction.[51] To the degree that other circuits disagree with the Second Circuit's interpretation of their cases here, though, *Cartoon Network* could presage a split of opinion within the federal district courts on the duration requirement for fixation.[52]

The Second Circuit did not reach Cablevision's suggestion that "any copies produced by buffering data would be de minimis."[53] Its failure to do so leaves open the possibility that future courts could find that buffer copies lasting longer than 1.2 seconds meet the duration requirement for fixation without being infringing reproductions.

Reproduction under the Copyright Act: The Agent of Copying with RS-DVRs

The *Cartoon Network* plaintiffs further claimed that Cablevision infringed their reproduction rights by creating unauthorized and unlicensed playback copies and saving them on Cablevision hard drives for future viewing by customers.[54] Whether these copies violated broadcasters' exclusive rights to reproduce their works was not at issue here.[55] Rather, the parties and the courts focused upon Cablevision's role in creating the playback copies.[56] This focus resulted from the fact that the plaintiffs claimed direct infringement by Cablevision, and liability for direct infringement exists only when the defendants' own conduct "violates any exclusive rights of the copyright owner."[57] If the defendants' own conduct does not violate an exclusive right, there can be no direct liability.[58] There can only be contributory or vicarious liability, or liability for any infringing conduct by third parties, which the parties had agreed not to assert here.[59] The key question thus became whether Cablevision or its customers made the playback copies.

The plaintiffs argued, and the district court agreed, that Cablevision made the copies and should be directly liable for infringement because the copies were unauthorized and unlicensed.[60] Technological differences between VCRs, STS-DVRs and RS-DVRs were key to this argument.[61] The plaintiffs claimed that RS-DVRs differed from earlier time-shifting technologies because they were not stand-alone devices that consumers purchased and installed in their homes.[62] Relatedly, plaintiffs claimed that RS-DVRs were different because Cablevision had an "ongoing participation" in the recording process because customers repeatedly transmitted recording requests to Cablevision's systems, which made and stored desired copies for them.[63] These differences convinced the district court that Cablevision's proposed RS-DVR offering was more like a Video-on-Demand (VOD) *service*, such as pay-per-view, which licenses all content it transmits and whose programs cannot be recorded on DVRs,[64] than a VCR *device*, used for recording broadcast television.[65] The district court thus found that Cablevision should be directly liable for copyright infringement.[66]

Cablevision had argued that it (1) merely provided copying equipment on its premises for customer use, like a store with customer-operated photocopiers, and (2) its customers made the playback copies because their requests initiated the copying.[67]

Because the Second Circuit saw no fundamental difference between RS-DVRs and VCRs, it held that Cablevision's customers made the unauthorized and unlicensed playback copies.[68] The fact that customer actions—such as selecting shows for recording via remote controls and entering the commands to record—were necessary precursors to the making of playback copies by Cablevision's system was key to this holding.[69] The Second Circuit further differentiated between (1) selling access to systems that automatically produce copies on command and (2) manually operating copying devices and selling products made using the devices:

> In determining who actually "makes" a copy, a significant difference exists between making a request to a human employee, who then volitionally operates the copying system to make the copy, and issuing a command directly to a system, which automatically obeys commands and engages in no volitional conduct.[70]

Public Performance under the Copyright Act: The Agent of Transmission with RS-DVRs and the Meaning of "Publicly"

In addition to their claim of infringing reproduction, the plaintiffs also argued that Cablevision infringed their copyrights by publicly performing their motion pictures and other audiovisual works.[71] The Copyright Act specifies that to "perform" a motion picture or other audiovisual work means "to show its images in any sequence or to make the sounds accompanying it audible."[72] The act further specifies that "publicly," when used in reference to performing a work publicly, means

> 1) to perform or display it at a place open to the public or at any place where a substantial number of persons outside the normal circle of a family and its social acquaintances is gathered; or
> 2) to transmit or otherwise communicate a performance or display of the work to a place specified by clause (1) or to the public, by means of any device or process, whether the members of the public capable of receiving the performance are in the same

place or in separate places and at the same time or different times.[73]

The plaintiffs argued that Cablevision's unauthorized and unlicensed transmission of playback copies to RS-DVR customers was infringing under these definitions of "performance" and "publicly."[74] According to the plaintiffs, the transmissions were (1) *performances* because they showed the images comprising the programming in the same order in which the images were originally broadcast and (2) *public* because numerous people were capable of receiving the same broadcast content in different places at different times.[75] Cablevision did not contest that the transmissions resulted in the performance of plaintiffs' copyrighted works.[76] Rather, it argued that Cablevision's customers—not Cablevision—initiated the performances because the RS-DVR system only sent the recorded programs to consumers upon their request for playback.[77] Cablevision also argued that any performance, regardless of who initiated it, was not public because each customer viewed "a distinct copy of a program uniquely associated with one customer's set-top box and intended for that customer's exclusive viewing in his or her home."[78]

The district court disagreed with Cablevision on both who initiated the performance of playback copies transmitted to RS-DVR customers and what makes a performance public.[79] The district court held that Cablevision was the agent of the performances because Cablevision "actively participated in the playback process" when its computerized system transmitted the playback copies to consumers upon their request.[80] It further found that the customers' participation in the transmission of the playback copies—their use of remote controls to select previously recorded content for viewing—was "too passive" for them to be the agents of the performance.[81] Finally, the district court held that the performances were public because multiple Cablevision customers received transmissions of the same shows.[82]

The Second Circuit reversed the district court on the question of whether unauthorized transmission of playback copies to RS-DVR customers constituted infringing public performances.83 The Second Circuit did so without deciding whether Cablevision or its customers initiated the performance.84 Rather, the court held that the performance was not "public" because different RS-DVR customers received individualized playback copies of the same television show.[85] The court found it significant that there was not a single playback copy transmitted to all subscribers who selected a particular show for recording and replay.[86] To the contrary, Cablevision ensured that each subscriber received a copy of the show viewable only on his or her set-top device.[87] This limitation, according to the Second Circuit, ensured that both factors used in determining whether a performance is public were unmet here: (1) the identity of the transmitter differed because the transmissions were made from different hard-drive storage spaces in response to commands from different customer remote-control devices, and (2) the source material of the transmission differed because the system saved individual copies of a program for each customer who requested recording of that program.[88] The Second Circuit's focus on this limitation does, however, raise questions about whether RS-DVRs must use Cablevision's allegedly "inefficient" method of recording content—which entails making and storing potentially thousands of copies of the same content—in order to avoid infringing the reproduction right.[89]

EFFECTS OF THE *CARTOON NETWORK* DECISION

The Second Circuit's decision, coupled with the Supreme Court's subsequent denial of certiorari in the case,[90] clears the way for Cablevision to deploy its proposed RS-DVR service commercially by protecting the latest in a line of technologies—stretching from VCRs to STSDVRs to RS-DVRs—that allow consumers to time-shift their viewing of broadcast television.[91]

A few questions remain after the *Cartoon Network* decision, however. First, the *Cartoon Network* plaintiffs and defendants declined to pursue claims relating to contributory infringement, vicarious infringement, or fair use.[92] Had they done so, the outcome on one or more of the three issues decided might have differed. Second, the *Cartoon Network* decision is a binding precedent only in the Second Circuit. Other federal circuits could potentially reach different conclusions on the nature of infringing reproductions and public performances under the Copyright Act even when confronted with identical facts.[93]

CONCLUSION

The Second Circuit's decision in *Cartoon Network* represents the latest in the continuing litigation between parties holding copyrights in broadcast programming and manufacturers of recording devices. *Cartoon Network* involved RS-DVRs and claims of direct infringement, unlike earlier cases involving VCRs or STS-DVRs and claims of contributory or vicarious infringement. Although the district court found for the plaintiffs and enjoined Cablevision from operating its proposed RS-DVR service, the Second Circuit reversed. The Second Circuit held that (1) the buffer copies created prior to recording broadcast content in Cablevision's RS-DVR system were non-infringing because they did not exist long enough for "fixation" under the Copyright Act; (2) the playback copies created on Cablevision's computers in its RS-DVR system did not make Cablevision directly liable for infringement because Cablevision's customers created them; and (3) the transmission of playback copies to customers was non-infringing because it was not a public performance. The Second Circuit's decision thus allows Cablevision to offer its proposed RS-DVR system commercially and clarifies the nature of infringing reproduction and public performance under the Copyright Act.

End Notes

[1] Cartoon Network LP, LLLP v. CSC Holdings, Inc., 536 F.3d 121 (2d Cir. 2008), rev'g Twentieth Century Fox Film Corp. v. Cablevision Sys. Corp., 478 F. Supp. 2d 607, 624 (S.D.N.Y. 2007). CSC Holdings is Cablevision's operating company. Company Overview: CSC Holdings, Inc., Hoover's (2008), available at http://www.hoovers.com/cscholdings/—ID__108770—/free-co-factsheet.xhtml.

[2] 17 U.S.C. § 106 (1) & (4).

[3] Cartoon Network, 536 F.3d at 124. Copyright holders involved in the Cartoon Network litigation were the Cartoon Network, CNN, Twentieth Century Fox, Universal City Studio, Paramount, Disney, CBS, ABC, and NBC. Id. at 121- 22.

[4] Twentieth Century Fox, 478 F. Supp. 2d at 624.

[5] How VCRs Work, How Stuff Works (2008), available at http://electronics. howstuffworks. com/vcr.htm.

[6] Sony Corp. of Am. v. Universal City Studios, Inc., 464 U.S. 417 (1984).

[7] Id. at 447.

[8] Id. at 452-53.

[9] Id. at 420.

[10] Id. at 447-55.

[11] Id. at 442.

[12] How DVRs Work, How Stuff Works (2008), available at http://electronics. Howstuffworks. com/dvr.htm.

[13] Complaint, Paramount Pictures Corp. v. ReplayTV, Case Number: 2:01-CV-09358-FMC-E (C.D. Cal. 2001), at 9.

[14] Id. at 14.

[15] Id. at 57-72. Plaintiffs' claim of contributory infringement was premised on the allegations that ReplayTV and SonicBlue (1) knew, or had reason to know, that consumers violated plaintiffs' reproduction and distribution rights when consumers used STS-DVRs to make unauthorized copies of plaintiffs' shows and (2) actively participated in consumers'

infringement by inducing, causing, or contributing to it by making STS-DVRs available to consumers. Plaintiffs' claim of vicarious infringement was similarly premised on the allegations that defendants (1) had direct financial interests in consumers' infringement, because they sold STS-DVRs to consumers, and (2) were able to control consumers' infringing recording, even if they did not know of or directly participate in it, because they determined the technological capabilities of the devices they manufactured.

[16] Newmark v. Turner Broad. Network, 226 F. Supp. 2d 1215, 1223 (2002) (granting consolidation of consumers' suit with the ReplayTV suit).

[17] Final Judgment, Paramount Pictures Corp. v. ReplayTV, Case Number: CV 01-09358 FMC (Ex) (S.D.N.Y. Aug. 25, 2006), at 1 (granting dismissal by stipulation of the parties).

[18] Cablevision, Products and Services, 2008, available at http://www.cablevision.com/.

[19] See, e.g., Larry Neumeister, Court Win for Remote Storage DVR, The Seattle Times, Aug. 5, 2008, at E1; John Consoli, Magna: DVR Usage Climbs, 18 Mediaweek 10 (2008).

[20] See, e.g., Declaration of Stephanie Mitchko in Support of Defendants' Motion for Summary Judgment, Twentieth Century Fox Film Corp. v. Cablevision Sys. Corp. (C.D. Cal. 2006), at 29 ("[I]f 1000 customers elect to record the February 25th 9:00 p.m. showing of Desperate Housewives, 1000 separate and distinct copies of that specific showing are made, each copy uniquely associated by identifiers with the set-top box of the customer who made the copy.").

[21] Cartoon Network, 536 F.3d at 124.

[22] Id.

[23] Id.

[24] Id.

[25] Id.

[26] Id. at 125.

[27] Id. at 124.

[28] Id.

[29] Id.

[30] Id.

[31] Twentieth Century Fox, 478 F. Supp. 2d at 621-22, 624.

[32] Cartoon Network, 536 F.3d at 126-40.

[33] 17 U.S.C. § 106(1).

[34] 17 U.S.C. § 101.

[35] Id.

[36] Id.

[37] See, e.g., Melville B. Nimmer & David Nimmer, 2 Nimmer on Copyright § 8.02 (2006) (discussing embodiment and duration in relation to the reproduction right); U.S. Copyright Office, DMCA Section 104 Report 109-114 (2001), available at http://www.copyright.gov/reports/studies/dmca/sec-104-report-vol-1.pdf (same).

[38] Cartoon Network, 536 F.3d at 127-30; Twentieth Century Fox, 478 F. Supp. 2d at 621-22.

[39] Cartoon Network, 536 F.3d at 129 (noting that embodiment in a medium occurs whenever a work is capable of being copied from that medium for any amount of time).

[40] Id. at 128; Twentieth Century Fox, 478 F. Supp. 2d at 621-22.

[41] Twentieth Century Fox, 478 F. Supp. 2d at 621-22.

[42] Id. ("[T]emporary copies ... are generally 'fixed' within the scope of the copyright owner's right of reproduction, so long as they exist for a sufficient amount of time to be capable of being copied, perceived or communicated.").

[43] Id. at 621.

[44] Cartoon Network, 536 F.3d at 130.

[45] Twentieth Century Fox, 478 F. Supp. 2d at 621.

[46] Cartoon Network, 536 F.3d at 129-30.

[47] Id.

[48] See, e.g., Stefan Hubanov, The Multifaceted Nature and Problematic Status of Fixation in U.S. Copyright Law, 11 Intell. Prop. L. Bull. 111 (2006); Douglas J. Masson, Fixation on Fixation: Why Imposing Old Copyright Law on New Technology Will Not Work, 71 Ind. L. J. 1049 (1996).

[49] See, e.g., Stenograph L.L.C. v. Bossard Assoc., Inc., 144 F.3d 96, 100 (D.C. Cir. 1998); Triad Sys. Corp. v. Southeastern Express Co., 64 F.3d 1330, 1335 (9th Cir. 1995); MAI Systems Corp. v. Peak Computer, Inc., 991 F.2d 511, 518 (9th Cir. 1993); Marobie-FL., Inc. v. Nat'l Ass'n of Fire Equip. Distribs., 983 F. Supp. 1167, 1177-78 (N.D. Ill. 1997). Because RAM is a "volatile" form of computer memory, whose content is lost if power is switched off and which can be overwritten, it is like a buffer in temporarily storing data. How RAM Works, How Stuff Works (2008), available at http://computer.howstuffworks.com/ram3.htm.

[50] MAI Sys., 911 F.2d at 518.

[51] Cartoon Network, 536 F.3d at 128 (noting that the program in MAI was in RAM for seven minutes and stating "[w]e construe MAI Systems and its progeny as holding that loading a program into a computer's RAM can result in copying").

[52] A recent District of Arizona case could allow the Ninth Circuit to reestablish the view that the time necessary for embodiment is per se more than transitory. See MDY Indus., LLC v. Blizzard Ent., Inc., 2008 U.S. Dist. LEXIS 53988 (D. Az. July 14, 2008), at *11 (relying on MAI Systems in concluding that a copy stored in RAM for at least several seconds is sufficiently fixed to constitute a "copy" and an infringing reproduction under the Copyright Act).

[53] Cartoon Network, 536 F.3d at 130.

[54] Twentieth Century Fox, 478 F. Supp. 2d at 617-21.

[55] Cartoon Network, 536 F.3d at 130.

[56] Cartoon Network, 536 F.3d at 130-33; Twentieth Century Fox, 478 F. Supp. 2d at 617-21. By comparison, there was no dispute as to whether Cablevision made the buffer copies. See Cartoon Network, 536 F.3d at 127.

[57] 17 U.S.C. § 501(a). Defendants' violation need not be knowing or intentional. Copyright infringement is a strict liability offense in that persons engaging in unlawful conduct are liable even without having specific knowledge or intent. Even strict liability offenses, however, require volitional conduct by the defendant for a finding of culpability. Cartoon Network, 536 F.3d at 133.

[58] Cartoon Network, 536 F.3d at 130.

[59] Id. at 124.

[60] Twentieth Century Fox, 478 F. Supp. 2d at 618.

[61] Id. at 618 ("[A]part from their time-saving functions, the RS-DVR and the VCR have little in common.").

[62] Id. ("The RS-DVR does not have that stand-alone quality.").

[63] Id. at 619.

[64] See, e.g., RCN Corporation, DVR User Manual: Frequently Asked Questions, 2008, available at http://www.rcn.com/cabletv/digital-video-recorder/faqs.php.

[65] Twentieth Century Fox, 478 F. Supp. 2d at 611, 619-20. The court further noted that Cablevision's RS-DVR system was developed from a modified VOD platform.

[66] Id. at 621.

[67] Id. at 617-18.

[68] Cartoon Network, 536 F.3d at 133.

[69] Id. at 131 ("[The] person who actually presses the button to make the recording ... supplies the necessary element of volition.").

[70] Id.

[71] Id. at 134-39; Twentieth Century Fox, 478 F. Supp. 2d at 622-24. The Copyright Act defines "motion pictures" as "audiovisual works consisting of a series of related images which, when shown in succession, impart an impression of motion, together with accompanying sounds, if any." 17 U.S.C. § 101. It further defines "audiovisual works" as "works that consist of a series of related images which are intrinsically intended to be shown by the use of machines, or devices such as projectors, viewers, or electronic equipment, together with accompanying sounds, if any, regardless of the nature of the material objects, such as films or tapes, in which the works are embodied." Id.

[72] 17 U.S.C. § 101.

[73] Id.

[74] Cartoon Network, 536 F.3d at 134.

[75] Id.

[76] Id. ("No one disputes that RS-DVR playback results in the transmission of a performance of a work.").

[77] Id.

[78] Id. at 138; see also Twentieth Century Fox, 478 F. Supp. 2d at 622.

[79] Twentieth Century Fox, 478 F. Supp. 2d at 622-24.

[80] Id. at 622. The district court specifically likened Cablevision's conduct in transmitting the playback copies to customers to that of the video store owners in Columbia Pictures Industries, Inc. v. Redd Horne, Inc. In Columbia Pictures, the Third Circuit held that video store owners directly infringe the public performance rights in copyrighted works when they rent videos for customers to view in private, restricted-access booths within their stores. The defendants in Columbia Pictures placed tapes into VCR machines at the front of the store and transmitted the content of the tapes to separate viewing rooms within the store, where the tapes could be seen only by those who rented them. Columbia Pictures Indus. v. Redd Horne, Inc., 749 F.2d 154, 157 (3d Cir. 1984).

[81] Twentieth Century Fox, 478 F. Supp. 2d at 622.

[82] Id. at 622-23.

[83] Cartoon Network, 536 F.3d at 134-39.

[84] Id. at 134.

[85] Id.

[86] Id.

[87] Id. Cablevision transmits playback copies into all homes in the same "node," or cluster of subscribers, as the customer for whom they are made, but only the customer for whom the copies are made has the necessary "key" to decrypt and view them. Twentieth Century Fox, 478 F. Supp. 2d at 615-16.

[88] Cartoon Network, 536 F.3d at 138.

[89] Network DVR Matter Goes to Court, The Online Reporter, May 27, 2006, at 8 (describing Cablevision's recording system as "inefficient").

[90] The Cartoon Network plaintiffs had petitioned the Supreme Court for review of the Second Circuit's decision, but the Supreme Court denied this petition on June 29, 2009. See Brent Kendall, Supreme Court Clears Way for Cablevision DVR Service, Dow Jones Newswires, June 29, 2009.

[91] See, e.g., Cartoon Network, 536 F.3d at 140 (lifting the district court's injunction); Deborah Yao, Cablevision's Great DVR in the Sky, TechNewsWorld, Sept. 23, 2008 (noting that the Cablevision RS-DVR service will be available in early 2009).

[92] Cartoon Network, 536 F.3d at 124.

[93] For example, if the Ninth Circuit were to affirm its precedents suggesting that the time required for embodiment suffices to meet any duration requirements for fixation, a split of opinion between the Second and Ninth Circuits could exist. See, e.g., MAI Sys., 991 F.2d at 518; MDY Indus., LLC, 2008 U.S. Dist. LEXIS 53988.

In: Internet Television Streaming …
Editor: Meredith Lane
ISBN: 978-1-63321-723-2

Chapter 3

DECISION OF THE SUPREME COURT OF THE UNITED STATES IN THE CASE OF AMERICAN BROADCASTING COS., INC., ET AL. V. AEREO, INC.*

Syllabus

NOTE: Where it is feasible, a syllabus (headnote) will be released, as is being done in connection with this case, at the time the opinion is issued. The syllabus constitutes no part of the opinion of the Court but has been prepared by the Reporter of Decisions for the convenience of the reader. See *United States* v. *Detroit Timber & Lumber Co.,* 200 U. S. 321, 337.

SUPREME COURT OF THE UNITED STATES

Syllabus

AMERICAN BROADCASTING COS., INC., ET AL. *v.* AEREO, INC., FKA BAMBOOM LABS, INC.

CERTIORARI TO THE UNITED STATES COURT OF APPEALS FOR THE SECOND CIRCUIT

No. 13–461. Argued April 22, 2014—Decided June 25, 2014

* This is an edited, reformatted and augmented version of the official slip opinion as delivered by the U.S. Supreme Court on June 25, 2014.

The Copyright Act of 1976 gives a copyright owner the "exclusive righ[t]" to "perform the copyrighted work publicly." 17 U. S. C. §106(4). The Act's Transmit Clause defines that exclusive right to include the right to "transmit or otherwise communicate a performance . . . of the [copyrighted] work . . . to the public, by means of any device or process, whether the members of the public capable of receiving the performance . . . receive it in the same place or in separate places and at the same time or at different times." §101.

Respondent Aereo, Inc., sells a service that allows its subscribers to watch television programs over the Internet at about the same time as the programs are broadcast over the air. When a subscriber wants to watch a show that is currently airing, he selects the show from a menu on Aereo's website. Aereo's system, which consists of thousands of small antennas and other equipment housed in a centralized warehouse, responds roughly as follows: A server tunes an antenna, which is dedicated to the use of one subscriber alone, to the broadcast carrying the selected show. A transcoder translates the signals received by the antenna into data that can be transmitted over the Internet. A server saves the data in a subscriber-specific folder on Aereo's hard drive and begins streaming the show to the subscriber's screen once several seconds of programming have been saved. The streaming continues, a few seconds behind the over-the-air broadcast, until the subscriber has received the entire show.

Petitioners, who are television producers, marketers, distributors, and broadcasters that own the copyrights in many of the programs that Aereo streams, sued Aereo for copyright infringement. They sought a preliminary injunction, arguing that Aereo was infringing their right to "perform" their copyrighted works "publicly." The District Court denied the preliminary injunction, and the Second Circuit affirmed.

Held: Aereo performs petitioners' works publicly within the meaning of the Transmit Clause. Pp. 4–18.

(a) Aereo "perform[s]." It does not merely supply equipment that allows others to do so. Pp. 4–10.

(1) One of Congress' primary purposes in amending the Copyright Act in 1976 was to overturn this Court's holdings that the activities of community antenna television (CATV) providers fell outside the Act's scope. In *Fortnightly Corp.* v. *United Artists Television, Inc.*, 392 U. S. 390, the Court determined that a CATV provider was more like a viewer than a broadcaster, because its system "no more than enhances the viewer's capacity to receive the broadcaster's signals [by] provid[ing] a well-located antenna with an efficient connection to the viewer's television set." *Id.,* at 399. Therefore, the Court

concluded, a CATV provider did not perform publicly. The Court reached the same determination in respect to a CATV provider that retransmitted signals from hundreds of miles away in *Teleprompter Corp.* v. *Columbia Broadcasting System, Inc.*, 415 U. S. 394. "The reception and rechanneling of [broadcast television signals] for simultaneous viewing is essentially a viewer function, irrespective of the distance between the broadcasting station and the ultimate viewer," the Court said. *Id.,* at 408. Pp. 4–7.

(2) In 1976, Congress amended the Copyright Act in large part to reject the *Fortnightly* and *Teleprompter* holdings. The Act now clarifies that to "perform" an audiovisual work means "to show its images in any sequence or to make the sounds accompanying it audible." §101. Thus, *both* the broadcaster *and* the viewer "perform," because they both show a television program's images and make audible the program's sounds. Congress also enacted the Transmit Clause, which specifies that an entity performs when it "transmit[s] . . . a performance . . . to the public." *Ibid.* The Clause makes clear that an entity that acts like a CATV system itself performs, even when it simply enhances viewers' ability to receive broadcast television signals. Congress further created a complex licensing scheme that sets out the conditions, including the payment of compulsory fees, under which cable systems may retransmit broadcasts to the public. §111. Congress made all three of these changes to bring cable system activities within the Copyright Act's scope. Pp. 7–8.

(3) Because Aereo's activities are substantially similar to those of the CATV companies that Congress amended the Act to reach, Aereo is not simply an equipment provider. Aereo sells a service that allows subscribers to watch television programs, many of which are copyrighted, virtually as they are being broadcast. Aereo uses its own equipment, housed in a centralized warehouse, outside of its users' homes. By means of its technology, Aereo's system "receive[s] programs that have been released to the public and carr[ies] them by private channels to additional viewers." *Fortnightly*, *supra,* at 400.

This Court recognizes one particular difference between Aereo's system and the cable systems at issue in *Fortnightly* and *Teleprompter*: The systems in those cases transmitted constantly, whereas Aereo's system remains inert until a subscriber indicates that she wants to watch a program. In other cases involving different kinds of service or technology providers, a user's involvement in the operation of the provider's equipment and selection of the content transmitted may well bear on whether the provider performs within the meaning of the Act. But given Aereo's overwhelming likeness to the cable companies targeted by the 1976 amendments, this sole technological difference between Aereo and traditional cable companies does not make a critical difference here. Pp. 8–10.

(b) Aereo also performs petitioners' works "publicly." Under the Clause, an entity performs a work publicly when it "transmit[s] . . . a performance . . . of the work . . . to the public." §101. What performance, if any, does Aereo transmit? Petitioners say Aereo transmits a *prior* performance of their works, whereas Aereo says the performance it transmits is the *new* performance created by its act of transmitting. This Court assumes *arguendo* that Aereo is correct and thus assumes, for present purposes, that to transmit a performance of an audiovisual work means to communicate contemporaneously visible images and contemporaneously audible sounds of the work. Under the Court's assumed definition, Aereo transmits a performance whenever its subscribers watch a program.

What about the Clause's further requirement that Aereo transmit a performance "to the public"? Aereo claims that because it transmits from user-specific copies, using individually-assigned antennas, and because each transmission is available to only one subscriber, it does not transmit a performance "to the public." Viewed in terms of Congress' regulatory objectives, these behind-the-scenes technological differences do not distinguish Aereo's system from cable systems, which do perform publicly. Congress would as much have intended to protect a copyright holder from the unlicensed activities of Aereo as from those of cable companies.

The text of the Clause effectuates Congress' intent. Under the Clause, an entity may transmit a performance through multiple transmissions, where the performance is of the same work. Thus when an entity communicates the same contemporaneously perceptible images and sounds to multiple people, it "transmit[s] . . . a performance" to them, irrespective of the number of discrete communications it makes and irrespective of whether it transmits using a single copy of the work or, as Aereo does, using an individual personal copy for each viewer.

Moreover, the subscribers to whom Aereo transmits constitute "the public" under the Act. This is because Aereo communicates the same contemporaneously perceptible images and sounds to a large number of people who are unrelated and unknown to each other. In addition, neither the record nor Aereo suggests that Aereo's subscribers receive performances in their capacities as owners or possessors of the underlying works. This is relevant because when an entity performs to a set of people, whether they constitute "the public" often depends upon their relationship to the underlying work. Finally, the statute makes clear that the fact that Aereo's subscribers may receive the same programs at different times and locations is of no consequence. Aereo transmits a performance of petitioners' works "to the public." Pp. 11– 15.

(c) Given the limited nature of this holding, the Court does not believe its decision will discourage the emergence or use of different kinds of technologies. Pp. 15–17.

712 F. 3d 676, reversed and remanded.

BREYER, J., delivered the opinion of the Court, in which ROBERTS, C. J., and KENNEDY, GINSBURG, SOTOMAYOR, and KAGAN, JJ., joined. SCALIA, J., filed a dissenting opinion, in which THOMAS and ALITO, JJ., joined.

Opinion of the Court

NOTICE: This opinion is subject to formal revision before publication in the preliminary print of the United States Reports. Readers are requested to notify the Reporter of Decisions, Supreme Court of the United States, Washington, D. C. 20543, of any typographical or other formal errors, in order that corrections may be made before the preliminary print goes to press.

SUPREME COURT OF THE UNITED STATES

No. 13–461

AMERICAN BROADCASTING COMPANIES, INC., ET AL., PETITIONERS *v.* AEREO, INC., FKA BAMBOOM LABS, INC.

ON WRIT OF CERTIORARI TO THE UNITED STATES COURT OF APPEALS FOR THE SECOND CIRCUIT

[June 25, 2014]

JUSTICE BREYER delivered the opinion of the Court.

The Copyright Act of 1976 gives a copyright owner the "exclusive righ[t]" to "perform the copyrighted work publicly." 17 U. S. C. §106(4). The Act's Transmit Clause defines that exclusive right as including the right to

> "transmit or otherwise communicate a performance . . . of the [copyrighted] work . . . to the public, by means of any device or process, whether the members of the public capable of receiving the performance . . . receive it in the same place or in separate places and at the same time or at different times." §101.

We must decide whether respondent Aereo, Inc., infringes this exclusive right by selling its subscribers a technologically complex service that allows them to watch television programs over the Internet at about the same time as the programs are broadcast over the air. We conclude that it does.

I

A

For a monthly fee, Aereo offers subscribers broadcast television programming over the Internet, virtually as the programming is being broadcast. Much of this programming is made up of copyrighted works. Aereo neither owns the copyright in those works nor holds a license from the copyright owners to perform those works publicly.

Aereo's system is made up of servers, transcoders, and thousands of dime-sized antennas housed in a central warehouse. It works roughly as follows: First, when a subscriber wants to watch a show that is currently being broadcast, he visits Aereo's website and selects, from a list of the local programming, the show he wishes to see.

Second, one of Aereo's servers selects an antenna, which it dedicates to the use of that subscriber (and that subscriber alone) for the duration of the selected show. A server then tunes the antenna to the over-the-air broadcast carrying the show. The antenna begins to receive the broadcast, and an Aereo transcoder translates the sig- nals received into data that can be transmitted over the Internet.

Third, rather than directly send the data to the subscriber, a server saves the data in a subscriber-specific folder on Aereo's hard drive. In other words, Aereo's system creates a subscriber-specific copy—that is, a "personal" copy—of the subscriber's program of choice.

Fourth, once several seconds of programming have been saved, Aereo's server begins to stream the saved copy of the show to the subscriber over the Internet. (The subscriber may instead direct Aereo to stream the program at a later time, but that aspect of Aereo's service is not before us.) The subscriber can watch the streamed program on the screen of his personal computer, tablet, smart phone, Internet-connected television, or other Internet-connected device. The streaming continues, a mere few seconds behind the over-the-air broadcast, until the subscriber has received the entire show. See A Dictionary of Computing 494 (6th ed. 2008) (defining "streaming" as "[t]he process of providing a steady flow of audio or video data so that an Internet user is able to access it as it is transmitted").

Aereo emphasizes that the data that its system streams to each subscriber are the data from his own personal copy, made from the broadcast signals received by the particular antenna allotted to him. Its system does not transmit data saved in one subscriber's folder to any other subscriber. When two subscribers wish to watch the same program, Aereo's system activates two separate antennas and saves two separate copies of the program in two separate folders. It then streams the show to the subscribers through two separate transmissions—each from the subscriber's personal copy.

B

Petitioners are television producers, marketers, distributors, and broadcasters who own the copyrights in many of the programs that Aereo's system streams to its subscribers. They brought suit against Aereo for copyright infringement in Federal District Court. They sought a preliminary injunction, arguing that Aereo was infringing their right to "perform" their works "publicly," as the Transmit Clause defines those terms.

The District Court denied the preliminary injunction. 874 F. Supp. 2d 373 (SDNY 2012). Relying on prior Circuit precedent, a divided panel of the Second Circuit affirmed. *WNET, Thirteen* v. *Aereo, Inc.*, 712 F. 3d 676 (2013) (citing *Cartoon Network LP, LLLP* v. *CSC Holdings, Inc.*, 536 F. 3d 121 (2008)). In the Second Circuit's view, Aereo does not perform publicly within the meaning of the Transmit Clause because it does not transmit "to the public." Rather, each time Aereo streams a program to a subscriber, it sends a *private* transmission that is available only to that subscriber. The Second Circuit denied rehearing en banc, over the dissent of two judges. *WNET, Thirteen* v. *Aereo, Inc.*, 722 F. 3d 500 (2013). We granted certiorari.

II

This case requires us to answer two questions: First, in operating in the manner described above, does Aereo "perform" at all? And second, if so, does Aereo do so "publicly"? We address these distinct questions in turn.

Does Aereo "perform"? See §106(4) ("[T]he owner of [a] copyright . . . has the exclusive righ[t] . . . to *perform* the copyrighted work publicly" (emphasis added)); §101 ("To *perform* . . . a work 'publicly' means [among other things] to transmit . . . a performance . . . of the work . . . to the public . . . " (emphasis added)). Phrased another way, does Aereo "transmit . . . a performance" when a subscriber watches a show using Aereo's system, or is it only the subscriber who transmits? In Aereo's view, it does not perform. It does no more than supply equipment that "emulate[s] the operation of a home antenna and [digital video recorder (DVR)]." Brief for Respondent 41. Like a home antenna and DVR, Aereo's equipment simply responds to its subscribers' directives. So it is only the subscribers who "perform" when they use Aereo's equipment to stream television programs to themselves.

Considered alone, the language of the Act does not clearly indicate when an entity "perform[s]" (or "transmit[s]") and when it merely supplies equipment that allows others to do so. But when read in light of its purpose, the Act is unmistakable: An entity that engages in activities like Aereo's performs.

A

History makes plain that one of Congress' primary purposes in amending the Copyright Act in 1976 was to overturn this Court's determination that community antenna television (CATV) systems (the precursors of modern cable systems) fell outside the Act's scope. In *Fortnightly Corp.* v. *United Artists Television, Inc.*, 392 U. S. 390 (1968), the Court considered a CATV system that carried local television broadcasting, much of which was copyrighted, to its subscribers in two cities. The CATV provider placed antennas on hills above the cities and used coaxial cables to carry the signals received by the antennas to the home television sets of its subscribers. The system amplified and modulated the signals in order to improve their strength and efficiently transmit them to subscribers. A subscriber "could choose any of the . . . programs he wished to view by simply turning the knob on his own television set." *Id.,* at 392. The CATV provider "neither edited the programs received nor originated any programs of its own." *Ibid.*

Asked to decide whether the CATV provider infringed copyright holders' exclusive right to perform their works publicly, the Court held that the provider did not "perform" at all. See 17 U. S. C. §1(c) (1964 ed.) (granting copyright holder the exclusive right to "perform . . . in public for profit" a nondramatic literary work), §1(d) (granting copyright holder the exclusive right to "perform . . . publicly" a dramatic work). The Court drew a line:

"Broadcasters perform. Viewers do not perform." 392 U. S., at 398 (footnote omitted). And a CATV provider "falls on the viewer's side of the line." *Id.*, at 399.

The Court reasoned that CATV providers were unlike broadcasters:

> "Broadcasters select the programs to be viewed; CATV systems simply carry, without editing, whatever programs they receive. Broadcasters procure programs and propagate them to the public; CATV systems receive programs that have been released to the public and carry them by private channels to additional viewers." *Id.*, at 400.

Instead, CATV providers were more like viewers, for "the basic function [their] equipment serves is little different from that served by the equipment generally furnished by" viewers. *Id.*, at 399. "Essentially," the Court said, "a CATV system no more than enhances the viewer's capac- ity to receive the broadcaster's signals [by] provid[ing] a well-located antenna with an efficient connection to the viewer's television set." *Ibid.* Viewers do not become performers by using "amplifying equipment," and a CATV provider should not be treated differently for providing viewers the same equipment. *Id.*, at 398–400.

In *Teleprompter Corp.* v. *Columbia Broadcasting System, Inc.*, 415 U. S. 394 (1974), the Court considered the copyright liability of a CATV provider that carried broadcast television programming into subscribers' homes from hundreds of miles away. Although the Court recognized that a viewer might not be able to afford amplifying equipment that would provide access to those distant signals, it nonetheless found that the CATV provider was more like a viewer than a broadcaster. *Id.*, at 408–409. It explained: "The reception and rechanneling of [broadcast television signals] for simultaneous viewing is essentially a viewer function, irrespective of the distance between the broadcasting station and the ultimate viewer." *Id.*, at 408.

The Court also recognized that the CATV system exercised some measure of choice over what to transmit. But that fact did not transform the CATV system into a broadcaster. A broadcaster exercises significant creativity in choosing what to air, the Court reasoned. *Id.*, at 410. In contrast, the CATV provider makes an initial choice about which broadcast stations to retransmit, but then "'simply carr[ies], without editing, whatever programs [it] receive[s].'" *Ibid.* (quoting *Fortnightly*, *supra*, at 400 (alterations in original)).

B

In 1976 Congress amended the Copyright Act in large part to reject the Court's holdings in *Fortnightly* and *Teleprompter*. See H. R. Rep. No. 94–1476, pp. 86–87 (1976) (hereinafter H. R. Rep.) (The 1976 amendments "completely overturned" this Court's narrow construction of the Act in *Fortnightly* and *Teleprompter*). Congress enacted new language that erased the Court's line between broadcaster and viewer, in respect to "perform[ing]" a work. The amended statute clarifies that to "perform" an audiovisual work means "to show its images in any sequence or to make the sounds accompanying it audible." §101; see *ibid.* (defining "[a]udiovisual works" as "works that consist of a series of related images which are intrinsically intended to be shown by the use of machines . . . , together with accompanying sounds"). Under this new language, *both* the broadcaster *and* the viewer of a television program "perform," because they both show the program's images and make audible the program's sounds. See H. R. Rep., at 63 ("[A] broadcasting network is performing when it transmits [a singer's performance of a song] . . . and any individual is performing whenever he or she . . . communicates the performance by turning on a receiving set").

Congress also enacted the Transmit Clause, which specifies that an entity performs publicly when it "transmit[s] . . . a performance . . . to the public." §101; see *ibid.* (defining "[t]o 'transmit' a performance" as "to communicate it by any device or process whereby images or sounds are received beyond the place from which they are sent"). Cable system activities, like those of the CATV systems in *Fortnightly* and *Teleprompter*, lie at the heart of the activities that Congress intended this language to cover. See H. R. Rep., at 63 ("[A] cable television system is performing when it retransmits [a network] broadcast to its subscribers"); see also *ibid.* ("[T]he concep[t] of public performance . . . cover[s] not only the initial rendition or showing, but also any further act by which that rendition or showing is transmitted or communicated to the public"). The Clause thus makes clear that an entity that acts like a CATV system itself performs, even if when doing so, it simply enhances viewers' ability to receive broadcast television signals.

Congress further created a new section of the Act to regulate cable companies' public performances of copyrighted works. See §111. Section 111 creates a complex, highly detailed compulsory licensing scheme that sets out the conditions, including the payment of compulsory fees, under which cable systems may retransmit broadcasts. H. R. Rep., at 88 (Section 111 is primarily "directed at the operation of cable television systems and the terms and conditions of their liability for the retransmission of copyrighted works").

Congress made these three changes to achieve a similar end: to bring the activities of cable systems within the scope of the Copyright Act.

C

This history makes clear that Aereo is not simply an equipment provider. Rather, Aereo, and not just its subscribers, "perform[s]" (or "transmit[s]"). Aereo's activities are substantially similar to those of the CATV companies that Congress amended the Act to reach. See *id.,* at 89 ("[C]able systems are commercial enterprises whose basic retransmission operations are based on the carriage of copyrighted program material"). Aereo sells a service that allows subscribers to watch television programs, many of which are copyrighted, almost as they are being broadcast. In providing this service, Aereo uses its own equipment, housed in a centralized warehouse, outside of its users' homes. By means of its technology (antennas, trans-coders, and servers), Aereo's system "receive[s] programs that have been released to the public and carr[ies] them by private channels to additional viewers." *Fortnightly*, 392 U. S., at 400. It "carr[ies] . . . whatever programs [it] receive[s]," and it offers "all the programming" of each over-the-air station it carries. *Id.,* at 392, 400.

Aereo's equipment may serve a "viewer function"; it may enhance the viewer's ability to receive a broadcaster's programs. It may even emulate equipment a viewer could use at home. But the same was true of the equipment that was before the Court, and ultimately before Congress, in *Fortnightly* and *Teleprompter.*

We recognize, and Aereo and the dissent emphasize, one particular difference between Aereo's system and the cable systems at issue in *Fortnightly* and *Teleprompter*. The systems in those cases transmitted constantly; they sent continuous programming to each subscriber's television set. In contrast, Aereo's system remains inert until a subscriber indicates that she wants to watch a program. Only at that moment, in automatic response to the subscriber's request, does Aereo's system activate an antenna and begin to transmit the requested program.

This is a critical difference, says the dissent. It means that Aereo's subscribers, not Aereo, "selec[t] the copyrighted content" that is "perform[ed]," *post,* at 4 (opinion of SCALIA, J.), and for that reason they, not Aereo, "transmit" the performance. Aereo is thus like "a copy shop that provides its patrons with a library card." *Post,* at 5. A copy shop is not directly liable whenever a patron uses the shop's machines to "reproduce" copyrighted materials found in that library. See §106(1) ("exclusive righ[t] . . . to reproduce the copyrighted work"). And by the same token, Aereo should not be directly liable whenever its patrons use its equipment to "transmit" copyrighted television programs to their screens.

In our view, however, the dissent's copy shop argument, in whatever form, makes too much out of too little. Given Aereo's overwhelming likeness to the cable companies targeted by the 1976 amendments, this sole technological difference between Aereo and traditional cable companies does not make a critical difference here. The subscribers of the *Fortnightly* and *Teleprompter* cable systems also selected what programs to display on their receiving sets. Indeed, as we explained in *Fortnightly*, such a subscriber "could choose any of the . . . programs he wished to view by simply turning the knob on his own television set." 392 U. S., at 392. The same is true of an Aereo subscriber. Of course, in *Fortnightly* the television signals, in a sense, lurked behind the screen, ready to emerge when the subscriber turned the knob. Here the signals pursue their ordinary course of travel through the universe until today's "turn of the knob"—a click on a website—activates machinery that intercepts and reroutes them to Aereo's subscribers over the Internet. But this difference means nothing to the subscriber. It means nothing to the broadcaster. We do not see how this single difference, invisible to subscriber and broadcaster alike, could transform a system that is for all practical purposes a traditional cable system into "a copy shop that provides its patrons with a library card."

In other cases involving different kinds of service or technology providers, a user's involvement in the operation of the provider's equipment and selection of the content transmitted may well bear on whether the provider performs within the meaning of the Act. But the many similarities between Aereo and cable companies, considered in light of Congress' basic purposes in amending the Copyright Act, convince us that this difference is not critical here. We conclude that Aereo is not just an equipment supplier and that Aereo "perform[s]."

III

Next, we must consider whether Aereo performs petitioners' works "publicly," within the meaning of the Transmit Clause. Under the Clause, an entity performs a work publicly when it "transmit[s] . . . a performance . . . of the work . . . to the public." §101. Aereo denies that it satisfies this definition. It reasons as follows: First, the "performance" it "transmit[s]" is the performance created by its act of transmitting. And second, because each of these performances is capable of being received by one and only one subscriber, Aereo transmits privately, not pub- licly. Even assuming Aereo's first argument is correct, its second does not follow.

We begin with Aereo's first argument. What performance does Aereo transmit? Under the Act, "[t]o 'transmit' a performance . . . is to communicate it by any device or process whereby images or sounds are received beyond the place from which they are sent." *Ibid.* And "[t]o 'perform'" an audiovisual work means "to show its images in any sequence or to make the sounds accompanying it audible." *Ibid.*

Petitioners say Aereo transmits a *prior* performance of their works. Thus when Aereo retransmits a network's prior broadcast, the underlying broadcast (itself a performance) is the performance that Aereo transmits. Aereo, as discussed above, says the performance it transmits is the *new* performance created by its act of transmitting. That performance comes into existence when Aereo streams the sounds and images of a broadcast program to a subscriber's screen.

We assume *arguendo* that Aereo's first argument is correct. Thus, for present purposes, to transmit a performance of (at least) an audiovisual work means to communicate contemporaneously visible images and contemporaneously audible sounds of the work. Cf. *United States* v. *American Soc. of Composers, Authors and Publishers*, 627 F. 3d 64, 73 (CA2 2010) (holding that a download of a work is not a performance because the data transmitted are not "contemporaneously perceptible"). When an Aereo subscriber selects a program to watch, Aereo streams the program over the Internet to that subscriber. Aereo thereby "communicate[s]" to the subscriber, by means of a "device or process," the work's images and sounds. §101. And those images and sounds are contemporaneously visible and audible on the subscriber's computer (or other Internet-connected device). So under our assumed definition, Aereo transmits a performance whenever its subscribers watch a program.

But what about the Clause's further requirement that Aereo transmit a performance "to the public"? As we have said, an Aereo subscriber receives broadcast television signals with an antenna dedicated to him alone. Aereo's system makes from those signals a personal copy of the selected program. It streams the content of the copy to the same subscriber and to no one else. One and only one subscriber has the ability to see and hear each Aereo transmission. The fact that each transmission is to only one subscriber, in Aereo's view, means that it does not transmit a performance "to the public."

In terms of the Act's purposes, these differences do not distinguish Aereo's system from cable systems, which do perform "publicly." Viewed in terms of Congress' regulatory objectives, why should any of these technological differ- ences matter? They concern the behind-the-scenes way in which Aereo delivers television programming to its viewers' screens. They do not render Aereo's commercial objective any different from that of cable companies. Nor do they significantly alter the viewing experience of Aereo's subscribers. Why would a subscriber who wishes to watch a television show care much whether images and sounds are delivered to his screen via a large multisubscriber antenna or one small dedicated antenna, whether they arrive instantaneously or after a few seconds' delay, or whether they are transmitted directly or after a personal copy is made? And why, if Aereo is right, could not modern CATV systems simply continue the same commercial and consumer-oriented activities, free of copyright restrictions, provided they substitute such new technologies for old? Congress would as much have intended to protect a copyright holder from the unlicensed activities of Aereo as from those of cable companies.

The text of the Clause effectuates Congress' intent. Aereo's argument to the contrary relies on the premise that "to transmit . . . a performance" means to make a single transmission. But the Clause suggests that an entity may transmit a performance through multiple, discrete transmissions. That is because one can "transmit" or "communicate" something through a *set* of actions. Thus one can transmit a message to one's friends, irrespective of whether one sends separate identical e-mails to each friend or a single e-mail to all at once. So can an elected official communicate an idea, slogan, or speech to her constituents, regardless of whether she communicates that idea, slogan, or speech during individual phone calls to each constituent or in a public square.

The fact that a singular noun ("a performance") follows the words "to transmit" does not suggest the contrary. One can sing a song to his family, whether he sings the same song one-on-one or in front of all together. Similarly, one's colleagues may watch a performance of a particular play—say, this season's modern-dress version of "Measure for Measure"—whether they do so at separate or at the same showings. By the same principle, an entity may transmit a performance through one or several transmissions, where the performance is of the same work.

The Transmit Clause must permit this interpretation, for it provides that one may transmit a performance to the public "whether the members of the public capable of receiving the performance . . . receive it . . . at the same time or at different times." §101. Were the words "to transmit . . . a performance" limited to a single act of communication, members of the public could not receive the performance communicated "at different times." Therefore, in light of the purpose and text of the Clause, we conclude that when an entity communicates the same contemporaneously perceptible images and sounds to multiple people, it transmits a performance to them regardless of the number of discrete communications it makes.

We do not see how the fact that Aereo transmits via personal copies of programs could make a difference. The Act applies to transmissions "by means of any device or process." *Ibid.* And retransmitting a television program using user-specific copies is a "process" of transmitting a performance. A "cop[y]" of a work is simply a "material objec[t] . . . in which a work is fixed . . . and from which the work can be perceived, reproduced, or otherwise communicated." *Ibid.* So whether Aereo transmits from the same or separate copies, it performs the same work; it shows the same images and makes audible the same sounds. Therefore, when Aereo streams the same television program to multiple subscribers, it "transmit[s] . . . a performance" to all of them.

Moreover, the subscribers to whom Aereo transmits television programs constitute "the public." Aereo communicates the same contemporaneously perceptible images and sounds to a large number of people who are unre- lated and unknown to each other. This matters because, although the Act does not define "the public," it specifies that an entity performs publicly when it performs at "any place where a substantial number of persons outside of a normal circle of a family and its social acquaintances is gathered." *Ibid.* The Act thereby suggests that "the public" consists of a large group of people outside of a family and friends.

Neither the record nor Aereo suggests that Aereo's subscribers receive performances in their capacities as owners or possessors of the underlying works. This is relevant because when an entity performs to a set of people, whether they constitute "the public" often depends upon their relationship to the underlying work. When, for example, a valet parking attendant returns cars to their drivers, we would not say that the parking service provides cars "to the public." We would say that it provides the cars to their owners. We would say that a car dealership, on the other hand, does provide cars to the public, for it sells cars to individuals who lack a pre-existing relationship to the cars.

Similarly, an entity that transmits a performance to individuals in their capacities as owners or possessors does not perform to "the public," whereas an entity like Aereo that transmits to large numbers of paying subscribers who lack any prior relationship to the works does so perform.

Finally, we note that Aereo's subscribers may receive the same programs at different times and locations. This fact does not help Aereo, however, for the Transmit Clause expressly provides that an entity may perform publicly "whether the members of the public capable of receiving the performance . . . receive it in the same place or in separate places and at the same time or at different times." *Ibid.* In other words, "the public" need not be situated together, spatially or temporally. For these reasons, we conclude that Aereo transmits a performance of petitioners' copyrighted works to the public, within the meaning of the Transmit Clause.

IV

Aereo and many of its supporting *amici* argue that to apply the Transmit Clause to Aereo's conduct will impose copyright liability on other technologies, including new technologies, that Congress could not possibly have wanted to reach. We agree that Congress, while intending the Transmit Clause to apply broadly to cable companies and their equivalents, did not intend to discourage or to control the emergence or use of different kinds of technologies. But we do not believe that our limited holding today will have that effect.

For one thing, the history of cable broadcast transmissions that led to the enactment of the Transmit Clause informs our conclusion that Aereo "perform[s]," but it does not determine whether different kinds of providers in different contexts also "perform." For another, an entity only transmits a performance when it communicates contemporaneously perceptible images and sounds of a work. See Brief for Respondent 31 ("[I]f a distributor . . . sells [multiple copies of a digital video disc] by mail to consumers, . . . [its] distribution of the DVDs merely makes it possible for the recipients to perform the work themselves—it is not a 'device or process' by which the *distributor* publicly performs the work" (emphasis in original)).

Further, we have interpreted the term "the public" to apply to a group of individuals acting as ordinary members of the public who pay primarily to watch broadcast television programs, many of which are copyrighted. We have said that it does not extend to those who act as owners or possessors of the relevant product. And we have not considered whether the public performance right is infringed when the user of a service pays primarily for something other than the transmission of copyrighted works, such as the remote storage of content. See Brief for United States as *Amicus Curiae* 31 (distinguishing cloud-based storage services because they "offer consumers more numerous and convenient means of playing back copies that the consumers have *already* lawfully acquired" (emphasis in original)). In addition, an entity does not transmit to the public if it does not transmit to a substantial number of people outside of a family and its social circle.

We also note that courts often apply a statute's highly general language in light of the statute's basic purposes. Finally, the doctrine of "fair use" can help to prevent inappropriate or inequitable applications of the Clause. See *Sony Corp. of America* v. *Universal City Studios, Inc.*, 464 U. S. 417 (1984).

We cannot now answer more precisely how the Transmit Clause or other provisions of the Copyright Act will apply to technologies not before us. We agree with the Solicitor General that "[q]uestions involving cloud computing, [remote storage] DVRs, and other novel issues not before the Court, as to which 'Congress has not plainly marked [the] course,' should await a case in which they are squarely presented." Brief for United States as *Amicus Curiae* 34 (quoting *Sony*, *supra*, at 431 (alteration in original)). And we note that, to the extent commercial actors or other interested entities may be concerned with the relationship between the development and use of such technologies and the Copyright Act, they are of course free to seek action from Congress. Cf. Digital Millennium Copyright Act, 17 U. S. C. §512.

***

In sum, having considered the details of Aereo's practices, we find them highly similar to those of the CATV systems in *Fortnightly* and *Teleprompter*. And those are activities that the 1976 amendments sought to bring within the scope of the Copyright Act. Insofar as there are differences, those differences concern not the nature of the service that Aereo provides so much as the technological manner in which it provides the service. We conclude that those differences are not adequate to place Aereo's activities outside the scope of the Act. For these reasons, we conclude that Aereo "perform[s]" petitioners' copyrighted works "publicly," as those terms are defined by the Transmit Clause. We therefore reverse the contrary judgment of the Court of Appeals, and we remand the case for further proceedings consistent with this opinion.

It is so ordered.

Scalia, J., Dissenting

SUPREME COURT OF THE UNITED STATES
No. 13–461
AMERICAN BROADCASTING COMPANIES, INC., ET AL., PETITIONERS *v.* AEREO, INC., FKA BAMBOOM LABS, INC.
ON WRIT OF CERTIORARI TO THE UNITED STATES COURT OF APPEALS FOR THE SECOND CIRCUIT
[June 25, 2014]

JUSTICE SCALIA, with whom JUSTICE THOMAS and JUSTICE ALITO join, dissenting.

This case is the latest skirmish in the long-running copyright battle over the delivery of television programming. Petitioners, a collection of television networks and affiliates (Networks), broadcast copyrighted programs on the public airwaves for all to see. Aereo, respondent, operates an automated system that allows subscribers to receive, on Internet-connected devices, programs that they select, including the Networks' copyrighted programs. The Networks sued Aereo for several forms of copyright infringement, but we are here concerned with a single claim: that Aereo violates the Networks' "exclusive righ[t]"

to "perform" their programs "publicly." 17 U. S. C. §106(4). That claim fails at the very outset because Aereo does not "perform" at all. The Court manages to reach the opposite conclusion only by disregarding widely accepted rules for service-provider liability and adopting in their place an improvised standard ("looks-like-cable-TV") that will sow confusion for years to come.

I. Legal Standard

There are two types of liability for copyright infringement: direct and secondary. As its name suggests, the former applies when an actor personally engages in infringing conduct. See *Sony Corp. of America* v. *Universal City Studios, Inc.*, 464 U. S. 417, 433 (1984). Secondary liability, by contrast, is a means of holding defendants responsible for infringement by third parties, even when the defendants "have not themselves engaged in the infringing activity." *Id.*, at 435. It applies when a defendant "intentionally induc[es] or encourag[es]" infringing acts by others or profits from such acts "while declining to exercise a right to stop or limit [them]." *Metro-Goldwyn-Mayer Studios Inc.* v. *Grokster, Ltd.*, 545 U. S. 913, 930 (2005).

Most suits against equipment manufacturers and service providers involve secondary-liability claims. For example, when movie studios sued to block the sale of Sony's Betamax videocassette recorder (VCR), they argued that Sony was liable because *its customers* were making unauthorized copies. See *Sony, supra*, at 434–435. Record labels and movie studios relied on a similar theory when they sued Grokster and StreamCast, two providers of peer-to-peer file-sharing software. See *Grokster, supra*, at 920–921, 927.

This suit, or rather the portion of it before us here, is fundamentally different. The Networks claim that Aereo *directly* infringes their public-performance right. Accordingly, the Networks must prove that Aereo "perform[s]" copyrighted works, §106(4), when its subscribers log in, select a channel, and push the "watch" button. That process undoubtedly results in a performance; the question is *who* does the performing. See *Cartoon Network LP, LLLP* v. *CSC Holdings, Inc.*, 536 F. 3d 121, 130 (CA2 2008). If Aereo's subscribers perform but Aereo does not, the claim necessarily fails.

The Networks' claim is governed by a simple but profoundly important rule: A defendant may be held directly liable only if it has engaged in volitional conduct that violates the Act. See 3 W. Patry, Copyright §9:5.50 (2013).

This requirement is firmly grounded in the Act's text, which defines "perform" in active, affirmative terms: One "perform[s]" a copyrighted "audiovisual work," such as a movie or news broadcast, by "show[ing] its images in any sequence" or "mak[ing] the sounds accompanying it audible." §101. And since the Act makes it unlawful to copy or perform copyrighted works, not to copy or perform in general, see §501(a), the volitional-act requirement demands conduct directed to the plaintiff 's copyrighted material, see *Sony, supra,* at 434. Every Court of Appeals to have considered an automated-service provider's direct liability for copyright infringement has adopted that rule. See *Fox Broadcasting Co.* v. *Dish Network LLC*, 747 F. 3d 1060, 1066–1068 (CA9 2014); *Cartoon Network, supra,* at 130–131 (CA2 2008); *CoStar Group, Inc.* v. *LoopNet, Inc.*, 373 F. 3d 544, 549–550 (CA4 2004).[1] Although we have not opined on the issue, our cases are fully consistent with a volitional-conduct requirement. For example, we gave several examples of direct infringement in *Sony*, each of which involved a volitional act directed to the plaintiff 's copyrighted material. See 464 U. S., at 437, n. 18.

The volitional-conduct requirement is not at issue in most direct-infringement cases; the usual point of dispute is whether the defendant's conduct is infringing (e.g., Does the defendant's design copy the plaintiff 's?), rather than whether the defendant has acted at all (e.g., Did this defendant create the infringing design?). But it comes right to the fore when a direct-infringement claim is lodged against a defendant who does nothing more than operate an automated, user-controlled system. See, e.g., *Fox Broadcasting*, *supra*, at 1067; *Cartoon Network*, *supra*, at 131. Internet-service providers are a prime example. When one user sends data to another, the provider's equipment facilitates the transfer automatically. Does that mean that the provider is directly liable when the transmission happens to result in the "reproduc[tion]," §106(1), of a copyrighted work? It does not. The provider's system is "totally indifferent to the material's content," whereas courts require "some aspect of volition" directed at the copyrighted material before direct liability may be imposed. *CoStar*, 373 F. 3d, at 550–551.[2] The defendant may be held directly liable only if the defendant *itself* "trespassed on the exclusive domain of the copyright owner." *Id.,* at 550. Most of the time that issue will come down to who selects the copyrighted content: the defendant or its customers. See *Cartoon Network*, *supra,* at 131–132.

A comparison between copy shops and video-on-demand services illustrates the point. A copy shop rents out photocopiers on a per-use basis. One customer might copy his 10-year-old's drawings—a perfectly lawful thing to do— while another might duplicate a famous artist's copyrighted photographs—a use clearly prohibited by §106(1). Either way, *the customer* chooses the content and activates the copying function; the photocopier does nothing except in response to the customer's commands. Because the shop plays no role in selecting the content, it cannot be held directly liable when a customer makes an infringing copy. See *CoStar*, *supra,* at 550.

Video-on-demand services, like photocopiers, respond automatically to user input, but they differ in one crucial respect: *They choose the content.* When a user signs in to Netflix, for example, "thousands of . . . movies [and] TV episodes" carefully curated by Netflix are "available to watch instantly." See How [D]oes Netflix [W]ork?, online at http://help.netflix.com /en/node/ 412 (as visited June 20, 2014, and available in Clerk of Court's case file). That selection and arrangement by the service provider constitutes a volitional act directed to specific copyrighted works and thus serves as a basis for direct liability.

The distinction between direct and secondary liability would collapse if there were not a clear rule for determining whether *the defendant* committed the infringing act. See *Cartoon Network*, 536 F. 3d, at 132–133. The volitional-conduct requirement supplies that rule; its purpose is not to excuse defendants from accountability, but to channel the claims against them into the correct analytical track. See Brief for 36 Intellectual Property and Copyright Law Professors as *Amici Curiae* 7. Thus, in the example given above, the fact that the copy shop does not choose the content simply means that its culpability will be assessed using secondary-liability rules rather than direct-liability rules. See *Sony*, *supra*, at 434–442; *Cartoon Network*, *supra*, at 132–133.

II. APPLICATION TO AEREO

So which is Aereo: the copy shop or the video-on-demand service? In truth, it is neither. Rather, it is akin to a copy shop that provides its patrons with a library card. Aereo offers access to an automated system consisting of routers, servers, transcoders, and dime-sized antennae. Like a photocopier or VCR, that system lies dormant until a subscriber activates it. When a subscriber selects a program, Aereo's system picks up the relevant broadcast signal, translates its audio and video components into digital data, stores the data in a user-specific file, and transmits that file's contents to the subscriber via the Internet—at which point the subscriber's laptop, tablet, or other device displays the broadcast just as an ordinary television would. The result of that process fits the statutory definition of a performance to a tee: The subscriber's device "show[s]" the broadcast's "images" and "make[s] the sounds accompanying" the broadcast "audible." §101. The only question is whether those performances are the product of Aereo's volitional conduct.

They are not. Unlike video-on-demand services, Aereo does not provide a prearranged assortment of movies and television shows. Rather, it assigns each subscriber an antenna that—like a library card—can be used to obtain whatever broadcasts are freely available. Some of those broadcasts are copyrighted; others are in the public domain. The key point is that subscribers call all the shots: Aereo's automated system does not relay any program, copyrighted or not, until a subscriber selects the program and tells Aereo to relay it. Aereo's operation of that system is a volitional act and a but-for cause of the resulting performances, but, as in the case of the copy shop, that degree of involvement is not enough for direct liability. See *Grokster*, 545 U. S., at 960 (BREYER, J., concurring) ("[T]he producer of a technology which *permits* unlawful copying does not himself *engage* in unlawful copying").

In sum, Aereo does not "perform" for the sole and simple reason that it does not make the choice of content. And because Aereo does not perform, it cannot be held directly liable for infringing the Networks' public-performance right.[3] That conclusion does not necessarily mean that Aereo's service complies with the Copyright Act. Quite the contrary. The Networks' complaint alleges that Aereo is directly *and* secondarily liable for infringing their public-performance rights (§106(4)) *and also* their reproduction rights (§106(1)). Their request for a preliminary injunction—the only issue before this Court—is based exclusively on the direct-liability portion of the public-performance claim (and further limited to Aereo's "watch" function, as opposed to its "record" function). See App. to Pet. for Cert. 60a–61a. Affirming the judgment below would merely return this case to the lower courts for consideration of the Networks' remaining claims.

III. GUILT BY RESEMBLANCE

The Court's conclusion that Aereo performs boils down to the following syllogism: (1) Congress amended the Act to overrule our decisions holding that cable systems do not perform when they retransmit over-the-air broadcasts;[4] (2) Aereo looks a lot like a cable system; therefore (3) Aereo performs. *Ante,* at 4–10. That reasoning suffers from a trio of defects.

First, it is built on the shakiest of foundations. Perceiving the text to be ambiguous, *ante,* at 4, the Court reaches out to decide the case based on a few isolated snippets of legislative history, *ante,* at 7–8 (citing H. R. Rep. No. 94–1476 (1976)). The Court treats those snippets as authoritative evidence of congressional intent even though they come from a single report issued by a committee whose members make up a small fraction of one of the two Houses of Congress. Little else need be said here about the severe shortcomings of that interpretative methodology. See *Lawson* v. *FMR LLC*, 571 U. S. ___, ___ (2014) (SCALIA, J., concurring in principal part and concurring in judgment) (slip op., at 1–2).

Second, the Court's reasoning fails on its own terms because there are material differences between the cable systems at issue in *Teleprompter Corp.* v. *Columbia Broadcasting System, Inc.,* 415 U. S. 394 (1974), and *Fortnightly Corp.* v. *United Artists Television, Inc.,* 392 U. S. 390 (1968), on the one hand and Aereo on the other. The former (which were then known as community-antenna television systems) captured the full range of broadcast signals and forwarded them to all subscribers at all times, whereas Aereo transmits only specific programs selected by the user, at specific times selected by the user. The Court acknowledges this distinction but blithely concludes that it "does not make a critical difference." *Ante,* at 10. Even if that were true, the Court fails to account for other salient differences between the two technologies.[5] Though cable systems started out essentially as dumb pipes that routed signals from point A to point B, see *ante,* at 5, by the 1970's, that kind of service "'no longer exist[ed],'" Brief for Petitioners in *Columbia Broadcasting System, Inc.* v. *Teleprompter Corp.*, O. T. 1973, No. 72–1633, p. 22. At the time of our *Teleprompter* decision, cable companies "perform[ed] the same functions as 'broadcasters' by deliberately selecting and importing distant signals, originating programs, [and] selling commercials," *id.,* at 20, thus making them curators of content—more akin to video-ondemand services than copy shops. So far as the record reveals, Aereo does none of those things.

Third, and most importantly, even accepting that the 1976 amendments had as their purpose the overruling of our cable-TV cases, what they were meant to do and how they did it are two different questions—and it is the latter that governs the case before us here. The injury claimed is not violation of a law that says operations similar to cable TV are subject to copyright liability, but violation of §106(4) of the Copyright Act. And whatever soothing reasoning the Court uses to reach its result ("this looks like cable TV"), the consequence of its holding is that someone who implements this technology *"perform[s]" under that provision.* That greatly disrupts settled jurisprudence which, before today, applied the straightforward, bright-line test of volitional conduct directed at the copyrighted work. If that test is not outcome determinative in this case, presumably it is not outcome determinative elsewhere as well. And it is not clear what the Court proposes to replace it. Perhaps the Court means to adopt (invent, really) a two-tier version of the Copyright Act, one part of which applies to "cable companies and their equivalents" while the other governs everyone else. *Ante,* at 9– 10, 16.

The rationale for the Court's ad hoc rule for cable-system lookalikes is so broad that it renders nearly a third of the Court's opinion superfluous. Part II of the opinion concludes that Aereo performs because it resembles a cable company, and Congress amended the Act in 1976 "to bring the activities of cable systems within [its] scope." *Ante,* at 8. Part III of the opinion purports to address separately the question whether Aereo performs "pub- licly." *Ante,* at 10–15. Trouble is, that question cannot remain open if Congress's supposed intent to regulate whatever looks like a cable company must be given legal effect (as the Court says in Part II). The Act reaches only public performances, see §106(4), so Congress could not have regulated "the activities of cable systems" without deeming their retransmissions public performances. The upshot is this: If Aereo's similarity to a cable company means that it performs, then by necessity that same characteristic means that it does so publicly, and Part III of the Court's opinion discusses an issue that is no longer relevant—though discussing it certainly gives the opinion the "feel" of real textual analysis.

Making matters worse, the Court provides no criteria for determining when its cable-TV-lookalike rule applies. Must a defendant offer access to live television to qualify? If similarity to cable-television service is the measure, then the answer must be yes. But consider the implications of that answer: Aereo would be free to do exactly what it is doing right now so long as it built mandatory time shifting into its "watch" function.[6] Aereo would not be providing *live* television if it made subscribers wait to tune in until after a show's live broadcast ended. A subscriber could watch the 7 p.m. airing of a 1-hour program any time after 8 p.m. Assuming the Court does not intend to adopt such a do-nothing rule (though it very well may), there must be some other means of identifying who is and is not subject to its guilt-by-resemblance regime.

Two other criteria come to mind. One would cover any automated service that captures and stores live television broadcasts at a user's direction. That can't be right, since it is exactly what remote storage digital video recorders (RS–DVRs) do, see *Cartoon Network*, 536 F. 3d, at 124– 125, and the Court insists that its "limited holding" does not decide the fate of those devices, *ante,* at 16–17. The other potential benchmark is the one offered by the Government: The cable-TV-lookalike rule embraces any entity that "operates an integrated system, substantially dependent on physical equipment that is used in common by [its] subscribers." Brief for United States as *Amicus Curiae* 20. The Court sensibly avoids that approach because it would sweep in Internet service providers and a host of other entities that quite obviously do not perform.

That leaves as the criterion of cable-TV-resemblance nothing but th'ol' totality-of-the-circumstances test (which is not a test at all but merely assertion of an intent to perform test-free, ad hoc, case-by-case evaluation). It will take years, perhaps decades, to determine which automated systems now in existence are governed by the traditional volitional-conduct test and which get the Aereo treatment. (And automated systems now in contemplation will have to take their chances.) The Court vows that its ruling will not affect cloud-storage providers and cable-television systems, see *ante,* at 16–17, but it cannot deliver on that promise given the imprecision of its result-driven rule.

Indeed, the difficulties inherent in the Court's makeshift approach will become apparent in this very case. Today's decision addresses the legality of Aereo's "watch" function, which provides nearly contemporaneous access to live broadcasts. On remand, one of the first questions the lower courts will face is whether Aereo's "record" function, which allows subscribers to save a program while it is airing and watch it later, infringes the Networks' public-performance right. The volitional-conduct rule provides a clear answer to that question: Because Aereo does not select the programs viewed by its users, it does not perform. But it is impossible to say how the issue will come out under the Court's analysis, since cable companies did not offer remote recording and playback services when Congress amended the Copyright Act in 1976.

***

I share the Court's evident feeling that what Aereo is doing (or enabling to be done) to the Networks' copyrighted programming ought not to be allowed. But perhaps we need not distort the Copyright Act to forbid it. As discussed at the outset, Aereo's secondary liability for performance infringement is yet to be determined, as is its primary and secondary liability for reproduction infringement. If that does not suffice, then (assuming one shares the majority's estimation of right and wrong) what we have before us must be considered a "loophole" in the law. It is not the role of this Court to identify and plug loopholes. It is the role of good lawyers to identify and exploit them, and the role of Congress to eliminate them if it wishes. Congress can do that, I may add, in a much more targeted, better informed, and less disruptive fashion than the crude "looks-like-cable-TV" solution the Court invents today.

We came within one vote of declaring the VCR contraband 30 years ago in *Sony*. See 464 U. S., at 441, n. 21. The dissent in that case was driven in part by the plaintiffs' prediction that VCR technology would wreak all manner of havoc in the television and movie industries. See *id.*, at 483 (opinion of Blackmun, J.); see also Brief for CBS, Inc., as *Amicus Curiae*, O. T. 1982, No. 81–1687, p. 2 (arguing that VCRs "directly threatened" the bottom line of "[e]very broadcaster").

The Networks make similarly dire predictions about Aereo. We are told that nothing less than "the very existence of broadcast television as we know it" is at stake. Brief for Petitioners 39. Aereo and its *amici* dispute those forecasts and make a few of their own, suggesting that a decision in the Networks' favor will stifle technological innovation and imperil billions of dollars of investments in cloud-storage services. See Brief for Respondents

48–51; Brief for BSA, The Software Alliance as *Amicus Curiae* 5–13. We are in no position to judge the validity of those self-interested claims or to foresee the path of future technological development. See *Sony*, *supra*, at 430–431; see also *Grokster*, 545 U. S., at 958 (BREYER, J., concurring). Hence, the proper course is not to bend and twist the Act's terms in an effort to produce a just outcome, but to apply the law as it stands and leave to Congress the task of deciding whether the Copyright Act needs an upgrade. I conclude, as the Court concluded in *Sony*: "It may well be that Congress will take a fresh look at this new technology, just as it so often has examined other innovations in the past. But it is not our job to apply laws that have not yet been written. Applying the copyright statute, as it now reads, to the facts as they have been developed in this case, the judgment of the Court of Appeals must be [affirmed]." 464 U. S., at 456.

I respectfully dissent.

End Notes

[1] An unpublished decision of the Third Circuit is to the same effect. *Parker* v. *Google, Inc.*, 242 Fed. Appx. 833, 836–837 (2007) (*per curiam*).

The Networks muster only one case they say stands for a different approach, *New York Times Co.* v. *Tasini*, 533 U. S. 483 (2001). Reply Brief 18. But *Tasini* is clearly inapposite; it dealt with the question whether the defendants' copying was permissible, not whether the defendants were the ones who made the copies. See 533 U. S., at 487– 488, 492, 504–506.

[2] Congress has enacted several safe-harbor provisions applicable to automated network processes, see, e.g., 17 U. S. C. §512(a)–(b), but those provisions do not foreclose "any other defense," §512(*l*), including a volitional-conduct defense.

[3] Because I conclude that Aereo does not perform at all, I do not reach the question whether the performances in this case are to the public. See *ante,* at 10–15.

[4] See *Teleprompter Corp.* v. *Columbia Broadcasting System, Inc.*, 415 U. S. 394 (1974); *Fortnightly Corp.* v. *United Artists Television, Inc.*, 392 U. S. 390 (1968).

[5] The Court observes that "[t]he subscribers of the *Fortnightly* and *Teleprompter* cable systems . . . selected what programs to display on their receiving sets," but acknowledges that those choices were possible only because "the television signals, in a sense, lurked behind the screen, ready to emerge when the subscriber turned the knob." *Ante,* at 10. The latter point is dispositive: The signals were "ready to emerge" because the cable system—much like a video-on-demand provider— took affirmative, volitional steps to *put* them there. As discussed above, the same cannot be said of the programs available through Aereo's automated system.

[6] Broadcasts accessible through the "watch" function are technically not live because Aereo's servers take anywhere from a few seconds to a few minutes to begin transmitting data to a subscriber's device. But the resulting delay is so brief that it cannot reasonably be classified as time shifting.

INDEX

A

access, 3, 5, 7, 12, 13, 17, 26, 28, 34, 43, 45, 57, 60, 61
accessibility, 8
accountability, 57
Aereo, i, iii, v, vii, viii, ix, 1, 2, 3, 4, 5, 7, 8, 9, 10, 11, 12, 13, 14, 15, 16, 17, 18, 37, 38, 39, 40, 42, 43, 44, 47, 48, 49, 50, 51, 52, 53, 54, 55, 57, 58, 59, 60, 61, 62
ASL, 17
authority, 25

B

ban, 18
blogs, 17
boils, 58
broadcast networks, viii, 19
broadcast television, vii, 1, 2, 4, 8, 11, 13, 15, 22, 23, 27, 30, 39, 42, 45, 46, 49, 52, 61
broadcast television industry, 13
broadcasting companies, vii, 1
browser, 4

C

cable system, 39, 40, 44, 46, 47, 48, 50, 58, 59, 62
cable television, 14, 46, 47
cables, 44
Cablevision, viii, ix, 7, 9, 10, 13, 16, 17, 19, 20, 22, 23, 24, 25, 26, 27, 28, 29, 30, 31, 32, 33, 34, 35
case law, 26
CBS, 31, 61
cities, 44
City, 31, 53, 54
CNN, 31
commercial, 7, 12, 21, 47, 50, 53
commercials, 22, 59
communication, 6, 10, 12, 51
community, 38, 44, 58
competition, 15
composition, 9
computer, 23, 26, 33, 42, 49
computing, 53
conflict, 14
congress, viii, 1, 2, 4, 6, 10, 12, 13, 14, 15, 18, 19, 38, 39, 40, 44, 46, 47, 48, 50, 52, 53, 58, 59, 61, 62
consolidation, 32
constituents, 50
construction, 46

consumer choice, viii, 2, 15
consumers, viii, ix, 19, 20, 21, 22, 23, 27, 29, 30, 31, 32, 52, 53
consumption, 12
copyright claims, viii, 19, 21
copyright law, vii, 1, 3, 6
Court of Appeals, vii, ix, 2, 3, 6, 8, 14, 20, 53, 55, 62
creativity, 45
customers, ix, 8, 20, 21, 23, 24, 25, 27, 28, 29, 31, 32, 34, 55, 56
CV, 31, 32

D

dance, 6
defects, 58
defendants, 27, 30, 32, 34, 54, 57, 62
denial, ix, 8, 20, 21, 30
digital video recorders, vii, ix, 4, 20, 60
directives, 44
dissenting opinion, 41
distribution, 24, 31, 52
district courts, viii, 2, 11, 13, 17, 26
District of Columbia, viii, 2, 3, 11, 14

E

e-mail, 50
equipment, 22, 24, 28, 34, 38, 39, 44, 45, 47, 48, 55, 56, 60
evidence, 58
exercise, 55

F

fair use, ix, 20, 22, 30, 53
FilmOn, v, vii, viii, 1, 2, 3, 4, 5, 7, 11, 12, 14, 15, 16, 17, 18
films, 34
financial, 32
fixation, ix, 20, 25, 26, 27, 31, 35
FMC, 31, 32
Football, 14, 17
foundations, 58

G

grants, 25
guilt, 60

H

HE, 17
history, 10, 12, 13, 47, 52, 58
homes, 22, 23, 27, 34, 39, 45, 47
host, 60
hotel, 7
House, 10, 12
House Report, 10, 12
human, 28

I

ID, 31
identity, 30
images, 6, 9, 25, 28, 29, 34, 39, 40, 46, 49, 50, 51, 52, 55, 57
individuals, 51, 52
industries, 61
industry, 13, 14
injury, 59
internet television streaming, vii
investments, 61
issues, viii, 2, 13, 30, 53

L

laptop, 57
laws, vii, 6, 62
lawyers, 61
legality, 61
legislative proposals, 4
light, 44, 48, 51, 53
litigation, viii, 2, 3, 4, 13, 24, 30, 31

M

machinery, 48
MAI, 26, 33, 35
Major League Baseball, 14, 17
majority, 10, 61
manufacturing, 22
marketplace, 15
materials, 20, 48
matter, 50
media, 4, 6, 16
memory, 23, 26, 33
methodology, 58
mobile device, 2, 4
movie studios, viii, 19, 20, 22, 55
multiple interpretations, vii, 1, 3

N

Nimmer on Copyright, 32

O

operations, 47, 59

P

performers, 45
permission, 3
permit, 25, 51
photographs, 56
platform, 33
playing, 9, 53
PM, 17
precedent(s), ix, 20, 30, 35, 43
producers, 38, 43
profit, 44
programming, vii, viii, ix, 1, 2, 4, 5, 13, 15, 20, 21, 23, 24, 29, 30, 38, 42, 45, 47, 50, 54, 61
public domain, 57
public performance right, vii, viii, ix, 1, 2, 3, 7, 8, 9, 10, 11, 13, 19, 20, 23, 24, 34, 53

R

radio, 6
reading, 13, 26
real time, 23
reasoning, 13, 58, 59
reception, 39, 45
rendition, 12, 46
rent, 34
reproduction, viii, ix, 19, 20, 23, 24, 25, 26, 27, 28, 30, 31, 32, 33, 58, 61
requirements, 35
response, 15, 17, 30, 47, 56
restrictions, 50
retransmissions, vii, 2, 9, 11, 14, 60
rights, viii, ix, 5, 11, 19, 20, 21, 23, 24, 27, 31, 34, 58
rules, 54, 57

S

scope, vii, 1, 10, 11, 12, 13, 17, 32, 38, 39, 44, 47, 53, 59
secondary liability, 56, 61
self-interest, 62
servers, 42, 47, 57, 62
service provider, 55, 56, 60
services, 4, 14, 15, 23, 53, 56, 57, 59, 61
showing, 9, 12, 32, 46
signals, 12, 15, 38, 39, 43, 44, 45, 46, 48, 49, 58, 62
signs, 56
snippets, 58
social circle, 53
software, 26, 55
Solicitor General, 53
solution, 61
specific knowledge, 33
speech, 50
storage, vii, viii, ix, 7, 19, 20, 21, 23, 30, 53, 60, 61
stretching, 30
subscribers, vii, viii, 1, 2, 4, 5, 10, 12, 15, 23, 29, 34, 38, 39, 40, 42, 43, 44, 45, 46,

47, 48, 49, 50, 51, 52, 54, 55, 57, 58, 60, 61, 62
subscription fee, vii, 1, 2
succession, 34
supplier, 48
Supreme Court, i, iii, v, viii, ix, 2, 13, 14, 20, 21, 22, 24, 30, 34, 37, 41

T

technological developments, 14
technologies, vii, viii, ix, 1, 12, 19, 20, 21, 23, 27, 50, 53
technology, vii, viii, 1, 2, 3, 4, 7, 10, 11, 13, 14, 15, 16, 21, 39, 47, 48, 57, 59, 61, 62
telecommunications, 22
telephone, 23
television commercial, 22
television viewing, 22
tension, 14
transmission, viii, ix, 2, 6, 7, 8, 9, 10, 11, 12, 13, 14, 20, 23, 24, 25, 29, 31, 34, 40, 43, 50, 53, 56
treatment, 60
triggers, 9, 11
twist, 62

U

United, v, ix, 18, 37, 38, 41, 44, 49, 53, 58, 60, 62
United States, v, ix, 18, 37, 41, 49, 53, 60
universe, 48

V

video programming, 15
videos, 34
vote, 61

W

Washington, 41
watches, 4, 44
web, 4
web browser, 4